Keith G. Saire, CHA has built the reputation of being one of the leading experts in the many facets of the Hospitality Industry. Not only does he hold two degrees in the hospitality industry but also has earned the much-coveted CHA designation (Certified Hospitality Administrator). This certification is only awarded to those that have a proven track record of success, completed an intensive study and have undergone rigorous testing. He also was involved with residential real estate and financial planning, licensed by the State of Pennsylvania.

After moving to Orlando, Florida, Mr. Saire traveled the United States, successfully turning around poorly performing hotels and restaurants. In 2003 he decided to enter the field of Vacation Ownership and was considered a member of the Top Gun team at his previous resort with (at the time this writing began) a weekly APG of 6557, a score that shows success for him, his team and the resort he served. Due to this success, Mr. Saire was promoted to the Director of Sales (DOS) at his current home resort. He is currently overseeing and providing the same quality of service to the Resort Owners, Exchangers and Guests.

As a member of the Orlando Chamber of Commerce and the American Hotel and Lodging Association, he continues to feel the pulse of the hospitality industry. He has been a certified referral travel agent (CRTA) for several years as well as certified by the Cruise Line International Association (CLIA).

Mr. Saire is a great believer that to have faith in any knowledge you are about to learn, you first need faith in the person teaching you that knowledge. Thus a brief resume of his recent achievements would not be out of place at this time. Part of the reason for writing this book was to offer to others the life experiences he and his family enjoyed over the years.

Mr. Saire is always looking for a better way to share his knowledge and is available for private consultation, as a guest speaker and trainer.

SECRETS REVEALED BY A TIMESHARE INSIDER

How to Write Off Your Timeshare, Your Expenses and Your Vacations

Keith G. Saire, CHA

Order this book online at www.trafford.com
or email orders@trafford.com

Most Trafford titles are also available at major online book retailers.

Printed in the United States of America.

ISBN: 978-1-4251-3045-9 (sc)
ISBN: 978-1-4251-3046-6 (e)

Trafford rev. 10/19/2011

 www.trafford.com

North America & international
toll-free: 1 888 232 4444 (USA & Canada)
phone: 250 383 6864 ♦ fax: 812 355 4082

Dedication

So many have been involved in the writing of this book I find it impossible to thank everyone. If I left you out it was only due to spacing issues but know you will always have a special place in my heart. Let me begin by thanking Alexis for her untiring faith and patience in the writing of this book. I would not and could not have done it without you. To John and Arlene (dad and mom) for instilling the belief that time together is the greatest gift a parent can ever give. I don't remember what I got for Christmas last year but I remember our trip to Denver, Colorado, the Air Force Academy, Pikes Peak, Colorado Springs, the gold mine, the Pueblo Indian Cliff Dwellings, and the warmth of having my family and grandparents with me. To Carrie, Alison, Lauren and Jake for the reason families vacation. You have given more than you realize and I have received more than I can give. Thanks. To Kevin and Rick, memories go on and you are always with me as long as I remember the times. To all my friends, your influence made me who and what I am today. To the many peers I have had the pleasure working with over these many years: Carl Gatti, Steve Maciejczyk, Domenic Spirito, Paul Stevens, Bobby Siriani, Jerry May, David Cox, and Shawn Abbatessa for believing in me and giving me direction to be the best I can be. To Jack Reed, Ron Stricklin, Patt Heidle, Cappy, Mark Cardin, Pat Center, Richard Cloud, Glen Coltes, Nicole Daigle, Natalie Dickerson, Lourdes Edridge, Nash Fancy, Jaime Fare, Janice Fiore, Adel Hammami, Tammy Hughes, Tim Hurley, Al Lanichi, Tom Marflak, Dave Poppa, Brett Sadowski, Adam Smith, Bill Spear, Johnny Valentine Carroll and Chris Yawn for your faith and trust in me. You have given more than you will ever realize, have taught me more than anyone and have gotten closer than anyone was able to. Your guidance and help will never be forgotten.

To the IRS for the use of their public tax forms, Alexander Barbara, Lisa Ann Schreier, Rita M. Bruegger, Ben Gay III, TimeSharing Today and the American Resort Developers Association for their materials and invaluable information. To Harry Swart for his review of my materials to make sure all the information was current and correct at the time of this writing. And to the many, many timeshare owners I have helped become owners, you became part of my "timeshare" family, and to those who have taught me the many benefits and the clever ways to use timeshare, I am forever grateful. As always, if I can ever help in any way, never hesitate to email or call. May you be blessed as you continue to see the world through the eyes of others and experience life to its fullest. Ama Credi E Vai (Love, Believe and Go).

Become a T-R-A-V-E-L-E-R, not just a tourist.

Keith G. Saire, CHA

CONTENTS

Introduction

This book is written to educate and re-educate timeshare owners. It is also written to show you the "Secret" of Timeshare and the greatest tax benefits to be found by being a timeshare owner. You will learn how to use your timeshare as a "timeshare tax shelter." If you already own, and you want to skip to the end for the "secret" ok, but sometimes it helps to go back to the basics and see if you have forgotten anything along the way. If you currently do not own a timeshare, please read this cover-to-cover. I have deliberately left one side of each page blank so you can take notes along the way. Also please note at the time of this writing the Internal Revenue Service had not published all forms for the 2008 tax year. Some forms will be for 2007, however your tax adviser will be able to provide the latest forms. The Form number itself is correct, just not the current year. If you have any questions, you will find my personal email address at the end of the book or on the www.timesharetaxshelter.com web site. I have tried to keep it so simple my five-year old grandson Jake will understand (well sort-of). This is the way I explain this to current owners: If you need a doctor you don't call a lawyer, if you need a plumber, you don't call an electrician and if you want to "master" your timeshare, find a vacation consultant and learn from him/her. You see this maybe two to three times a year. A vacation consultant will see this two to three times a day. No offense intended but, who do you think should know a little more about timeshare vacations? If you said the vacation consultant, welcome to my world. And if you believe you need to talk to your lawyer, financial planner, accountant, mom or dad, brother or sister, uncle or aunt, your cousin, your bookie or priest (he said smiling . . . ok, maybe not your bookie or priest) before you become an owner, let me ask you one question: Are any of them going on vacation with you? If not, who are they to tell you how to travel and where to stay? This is something only you can decide. In my humble opinion, when they start paying for your vacations they can tell you how to vacation. Again, only you can decide what's best for you and your family. Good luck, good reading and I'll see you, "Traveler".

CHAPTER ONE

> The ant is knowing and wise, but he doesn't know
> enough to take a vacation.
> ~ Clarence Day

The success of timeshare over recent years is due to the amazing benefits and amenities it offers. However there is one main question you and only you can answer. "Is timeshare for you"? The rest of the information in this book won't matter if you can't use a timeshare. Save your money. However, if you enjoy at least one week of vacation each year (including all those weekend getaways), you greatly benefit by reading further.

Become a T-R-A-V-E-L-E-R instead of a tourist:

Timeshare
Resorts
Anytime, Anywhere
Value
Exchange
Luxury
Education
R you Ready for the Secret

Imagine the opportunity not only to own vacations for your lifetime and generations to come, but having the federal government pay you for it and hand you a deed. That's right! Take one minute and think about that . . . let it sink in . . . I'll wait . . . 3,2,1 . . .

Welcome back. I heard you saying to yourself, "Let me see if I understand what Keith just said . . . "I can own my vacations for life, leave a legacy of vacations to my children and the federal government will help me pay for it"! YES! The answer is YES, that is exactly what I said. But for now, let's decide if the choice should be to rent or own your vacations. There are many good books on the market about timeshares, how to buy them, how to use them, how to rent them, how to sell them . . . I'm not in competition here. I'm going to give you my opinions and some basic information. You decide for yourself if it makes sense. But if I can show you how you can own your vacations and have your accountant write them off I've done my job.

And please indulge just two more things. One, I have left each opposite page blank for you to take notes, make suggestions, plan your next adventure or any reason you may need the extra space. And two, let me say I believe strongly in Vacation Ownership. If things seem to be leaning a little to one direction, you are probably right. But do not let this sway your choice in any way. Again, if it doesn't make sense to you please don't go forward with ownership. I am not here to hurt you, only to show you another way. Life is about choice.

Here's the way I look at this. Do you own your own home? Renting is not such a bad idea. You cut a check each month and move on with your life. No worries. The landlord has to worry about the property taxes, insurance, upkeep, maintenance repairs, paying the mortgage, etc. So why do we decide to own instead of rent and take on all of these headaches? Because we feel we are throwing our money away. We can buy a home and make the same payments but they end after a few years. If you buy a home for $100,000.00 and pay back the $100,000.00 you now own it. Of course you have maintenance fees and taxes but that is ok. You own it. And imagine paying $100,000.00, living in your home for 20-30 years and selling it for $250,000.00. You have built equity in your real estate ownership and now have an asset. Which makes more sense to you?

Also, do you own your car or lease it? A lease is not a bad idea. You sign a contract and every month all you do is send a check. You have some maintenance fees to maintain the lease but every three years or so you trade the car back in and get a new one with the latest technology. You barely need to buy tires for this car. All you have to do is sign another contract and get a new one and continue to make those payments every month for the rest of your life. You may even be able to write off your car with the right circumstances. So why do we choose to buy our cars? Why do we pay $25,000.00 for a car that is worth $10,000.00 three years later? Because after we pay it off, it's ours. If we want to trade it in we can. If we want to hold it for ten years without making any payments we can. But the choice is ours!

Now I ask you, if you own your home, and own your car . . . why would you continue to "rent" your vacations? What do you have when you make those rent payments? You have receipts in a shoebox. (Remember, I told you in advance I lean toward ownership, but let's see if this is for you).

Let's begin . . .

CHAPTER TWO

"T" IS FOR TIMESHARE, IS IT FOR YOU?

> Vacation used to be a luxury, but in today's world it has become a necessity.
> ~Author Unknown

The Top Twenty Reasons to Consider Timeshare/Vacation Ownership

1. Full control of your vacations
2. Greater Health . . . Doctor Recommended . . . Feel Better, more Relaxed and Content
3. Quality Family Time with so many Amenity Options
4. Generations of Extraordinary Vacations (For Free?)
5. A Family Legacy of Worldwide Vacations
6. The Finest, most Luxurious, Fully-Equipped, Safest, Hassle-Free Accommodations Worldwide
7. You have 122 days off per year, where are you going?
8. Pride of ownership in Five-Star or Gold Crown accommodations. Everyday is a Holiday
9. Saving thousands of dollars over time
10. Traveling the world in safety . . . Hotels . . . certainly not!
11. Really, how comfortable can a hotel be?
12. Truly, home-like amenities for that "home-away-from-home" feel with spacious floor plans
13. Ownership with a Deed instead of renting with receipts
14. Comfort in knowing there is a place waiting for you; Just call or click
15. Save endless hours of research for next years trip
16. Your vacations and time are precious, why gamble with time and money
17. You are part of the fastest growing segment in the Hospitality and Leisure World
18. Reliving childhood memories and creating new ones
19. Greater income—Greater Wage Increases—A smarter way to vacation

20. No more unknown hotels, unexpected "surprises," paying to stay in a concrete "box" next to "Americas Most Wanted," the toilet flushing in the room next door is your morning alarm clock because of the cheap thin walls.

Now, use the old "Ben Franklin" approach to making a choice. Take a piece of paper and draw a line down the middle. On the Left side count how many reasons sound good to you. On the Right side count how many reasons don't. Now, answer each question honestly. No one else will know your answers, I promise. Be true to yourself. It's just this simple. If you have more in the YES column, start looking to own. If you have more in the NO column, then it's simple . . . this is not for you and your family. Don't own it. Continue to rent.

Note the example:
15 YES
5 NO

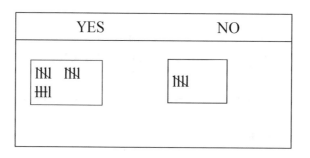

It's time to start looking toward ownership. Now what is the next step? With 52 Saturdays, 52 Sundays, 8 Holidays and 10 Vacation days off each year, what are you going to do with 4 months (122 days) off this year?

Ben Franklin's Decision Maker

Is Owning a Lifetime of Vacations For You?	Yes	No
1. Full control of your vacations		
2. Greater Health-Doctor Recommended-Feel better, more relaxed and content		
3. Quality family time with so many amenity options		
4. Generations of extraordinary vacations (for free?)		
5. A family legacy of Worldwide Vacations		
6. The finest, most luxurious, fully-equipped, safest, hassle-free accommodations worldwide		
7. You have 122 days off per year, where are you going?		
8. Pride of ownership in Five-Star or Gold Crown accommodations. Everyday is a Holiday		
9. Saving thousands of dollars over time		
10. Traveling the world in safety . . . hotels . . . certainly not!		
11. Really, how comfortable can a hotel be?		
12. Truly, home-like amenities for that "home-away-from-home" feel with spacious floor plans		
13. Ownership with a Deed instead of renting with receipts		
14. Comfort in knowing there is a place waiting for you. Just call or click.		
15. Save endless hours of research for the next trip.		
16. Your vacations and time are precious, why gamble with time and money		
17. You are part of the fastest growing segment in the Hospitality and Leisure World		
18. Reliving childhood memories and creating new ones		
19. Greater income—Greater wage increases—A smarter way to vacation		
20. No more unknown hotels, unexpected "surprises," paying to stay in a concrete "box" next to "Americas Most Wanted," the toilet flushing in the room next door is your morning alarm clock because of the cheap thin walls		
Total Your Answers Here ———————➤	Total Yes:	Total No:

CHAPTER THREE

"R" IS FOR RESORTS

> Year by year we are learning that in this restless,
> strenuous American life of ours vacations are essential.
> ~Ellsworth Huntington

As of 2005 there were over 5600 resorts worldwide. And it seems as though a new resort is opening somewhere on a weekly basis. Think about any country you would like to visit and almost any experience you would like to enjoy and timeshare will take you there. It's not as easy as closing your eyes and clicking your heels three times, but there is no place better to stay than a resort that feels like home.

There are several players in the timeshare resort exchange community. The two largest are Resort Condominiums International (RCI) and Interval International (II). Smaller companies include Platinum Interchange, Trading Places International, Hawaii Timeshare Exchange, Dial an Exchange and a few others. We will go into more detail on how you can trade up your exchanges later. For our purposes, we will just deal with the top two . . . RCI and II.

Just like hotels have ratings, so do timeshares. And just like hotels you have Five-Star down to budget. There are many different hotels available based on the income level of those needing them. But those staying in budget hotels today could very well be in Five-Star hotels in years to come. The same is true with timeshare. There are budget timeshares and Five-Star or Gold Crown resorts. Just like trading up your car or hotel chain, you can trade up your timeshare ownership based on affordability at the time in your life. It is affordable now for anyone who can afford to vacation one week a year.

As a side note: when you go to see a timeshare to consider a purchase keep in mind the sales representative has heard the word no in the past. Please, simply say no thank you. The old excuses of "I'm buying a home," "I'm buying a new car," "I'm saving for the kids college fund," "I have medical expenses/cancer/tumor/need surgery," "I'm filing for bankruptcy because I have too much debt," "I'm about to be laid off/changing jobs/unemployed," "I don't vacation," "This is my first vacation in years," "This will be my last vacation for years because . . . (fill in the blank)," "My dog/cat needs braces," (he says smiling again) and the many other excuses too numerous to list here, are just ways of saying no. Spare yourself the tension and politely say no and step away. Remember, with all these **standard** excuses that have been heard by the "reps" many times before, you are still on vacation spending your "much needed" money. The reps are compassionate and understanding and know not all those that come to see them are "misleading." However, after two to four presentations a day, five to six days a week, forty to sixty presentations per month the reps understand that you are spending "anyway money" and have become immune to those trying to "mislead" them. There is an ongoing joke in the industry that says there are only twenty reasons someone can give to say no. If you work long enough you will hear them over and over again. Just give the sales representative the truth and make it easy on both sides of the table. Neither side should feel tension when it comes to spending "anyway" money. The rep is there to make a living for their family, represent you to the company and will work to get the best deal for you and the company. This is what they do for a living. They are searching for a "meeting-of-the-minds" that becomes a win-win-win situation. Help them help you win! With that being said, let's move on.

There are many types of resorts. But how would you like to exchange your vacation for a Recreational Vehicle (RV) and drive around the world and see the sights? Or maybe boating is your dream vacation. You could exchange your vacation for a boat and travel the rivers in Europe or the Intercoastal Waterways in Florida. Yes, you can do this and more. Timeshare has expanded. You are no longer limited by your guidelines or tastes in what your ideal vacation will be. If your dream vacation is to go camping, use your timeshare, exchange and go camping. Already own an RV or camper/trailer? Good! Pull into thousands of sites and hook up at any facility coast-to-coast using your timeshare. Get a group of friends and family together and exchange for a catamaran and sail the Caribbean. And maybe every now and then, you have a want or need to stay in a city where there are no timeshare resorts. That's ok also. Exchange your timeshare and stay in a Five-Star or Gold Crown hotel. Timeshare is now flexible enough to be anything you need it to be.

In my personal opinion, if you can afford to do any of the above, you can't afford **not** to own timeshare. In the end it all goes back to Rent VS. Own. Would you rather have receipts or a deed to show for what you've spent? At least a timeshare is paid off with the same money you are spending anyway. That is why it is called "anyway money". You're going to spend the money **ANYWAY**! And here is one of the oldest arguments out there in timeshare land. Once your timeshare is paid off, you can vacation for free for the rest of your life. I can hear the Nay Sayers now from all over the world . . . all the way here in my private office. They are saying "What about the maintenance fees?" "What about any club dues?" "What about paying all those exchange fees?" Frankly, all good and legitimate questions! Let me give you an example to help you relate to maintenance fees. Let's say five years ago I approached you and offered you a card that **_guaranteed_** the opportunity to purchase fuel for your car at $1.00 per gallon. This card was going to cost you $5000.00 (Five Thousand Dollars) once, but it gave you the right to purchase all future fill-ups at $1.00 per gallon. Keep in mind, you are spending $5000.00 just for the right to make future purchases. Yes, you still have to pay

$1.00 per gallon for the fuel you buy! Knowing what you know now about the cost of fuel, and considering what it will cost five years from now, would you have bought my card? **In a second!** It would be worth every penny you spent. Isn't that the same about maintenance fees? You pay for your vacations once, only once and you travel the rest of your life and then leave it to others or sell it. And all you have to do is pay a small premium to maintain your purchase for future years to protect your investment in future vacations. Almost like a cheap insurance policy except you can use this policy without getting sick or dying like other insurance. You can collect on it every year.

Here is another way I answer the "fees" question. It all depends on the resort you own. Many resorts, for example, have an owner referral program set up to offset these costs. Developers will pay you to refer others to their resorts. This saves them marketing expenses and they would rather pay their owners instead of a marketing company. You have the ability of renting part of your ownership to offset. (Quick disclaimer here: No timeshare should ever be sold to you as an investment, it is about vacations. If someone promises you will make a fortune or fund your retirement, politely stand up, say no thank you and leave). I can and have rented my timeshare many times to offset the costs. So have some of my many owners. Can you do the same? YES! Will you? That frankly is up to you. But more on this later. Right now, suffice it to say you can do almost anything at any time in any way you need to use your timeshare ownership . . . always based on availability.

Many have asked me over the years, "but what about the accommodations?" I have a standard answer. "Even the worst resort is better than the best hotel room. The best hotel room is still one or two beds with a TV. If you're lucky, you get a recliner to sit in. My follow up question is: "Have you seen the TV show 'America's Most Wanted?' Where do all the criminals go when they are on the run? They can't go home because someone is waiting for them there and they can't get into resorts without being an owner or the guest of an owner. They need to go to hotels. Do you want to sleep down the hall from "America's Most Wanted"? Now I know you think this is a scare tactic, but step back and think about it for one minute. AM I RIGHT? Part of your maintenance fees is to pay for the luxury of 24/7 security. What security do you have at most hotels? I ran hotels as a Certified Hospitality Administrator (CHA) all over the country. I ask anyone to prove I'm wrong. Safety is a luxury you can afford.

One of the biggest benefits is having more than 5600 resorts to visit and enjoy worldwide. Accordingly, the Timeshare Users Group (TUG for short at www.tug2.net) and TimeSharing Today (www.timesharingtoday.com) are online communities established for independent timeshare owners offering ratings of resorts. The current most requested vacation spots are Orlando, Florida; the Florida coasts (both East and West); Las Vegas, Nevada; Hilton Head Island, South Carolina; and Myrtle Beach, South Carolina. There are many more locations in Europe such as Spain and the Canary Islands. Some locations are more suitable for certain ages such as kids and retirees. As per RCI, a few of the more popular vacation locations for retirees are the warm climates of Florida, Arizona, Marco Island, Colorado (before the snowfall), England, Italy and the Grand Caymans. Best destinations for families with children are Orlando, Florida, both East and West Florida coasts, Missouri, Texas, Williamsburg, Virginia, the Colorado Rockies for skiing and the Caribbean. But a timeshare may not be a location at all! You can exchange into a Yacht Club where you can sail a yacht or use your ownership to RV and exchange into campgrounds throughout the country. And finally, timeshare allows you to go all-inclusive and enjoy all the food, drink and entertainment you can handle or just take no trip at all. Go to a quiet location and unwind from the pressures and stress life throws at us. AHHHHH, timeshare, it offers something for everyone. Is it for you?

CHAPTER FOUR

"A" IS FOR ANYTIME AND ANYWHERE

> And that's the wonderful thing about family travel:
> it provides you with experiences that will remain
> locked forever in the scar tissue of your mind.
> ~Dave Barry

There are many different types of timeshare so before buying one you need to know the difference of each. This way you can do an informed comparison. Think of it like this, before you go to buy a house or rent an apartment you know in advance what you MUST have such as two or three bedrooms with one to three full baths, a full kitchen but maybe not a dining room if you do not plan to entertain often. Do you want a two story or everything on one floor? Before you buy a car you need to know in advance if you want a sedan, SUV or a convertible with or without the Satellite radio and GPS system. In the same way, know what you need before you go to buy a timeshare. There are three most common timeshare ownerships: fixed week, floating week and points. There are fractionals, which provide longer periods than one week at a time such as a twelfth-share, which means you own 4 weeks each year that may be used one week each season or a one-quarter share which could be used three weeks at a time in each of the four seasons of the year. You can also own different lengths of fractional time such as a quarter-share. This obviously depends on the amount you wish to spend on vacation. There are others, such as biennial (every other year), however I will only deal with the most common three here. Please permit me to add this disclaimer. Each ownership is correct for the person who owns it. Some like to go to the same place at the same time each year. Some travel to the same place but need a little more flexibility and others need to be completely flexible with their travel plans. No one way is better than the others as long as it provides what the owner is searching for with their travel plans.

Fixed week ownership is perfect for the traveler who enjoys going to the same place each year at the same time. An example of this would be someone wanting to visit a theme park in Orlando, Florida every Christmas holiday. They have no intention of using their ownership any other way, so a fixed week is exactly what they need. The point of fixed ownership is to guarantee that perfect vacation each and every time. Vacationing, however, is limited to that one week each year. If the traveler needs to cut a vacation short, they will lose the balance of their week. Ownership can never be used just to get away for a weekend.

A floating week means going to the same place each year but with more flexibility in time. If you enjoy visiting the same place, but cannot travel the same time each year, you need a floating week. Other than that this system is exactly the same as the fixed week.

The points program offers the most flexibility of all, allowing you to purchase the amount of points you need to travel as much or as little as you wish. These points "pay" for your vacation. On your anniversary date, you receive your points again. You can travel a few days at a time if you wish.

Look at it this way. Let's say you own 10,000 points and you want to spend 2000 points to take a vacation in Daytona Beach, Florida. When you make your reservation the company will deduct 2000 points from your total to pay for the trip. You still have 8000 points left to take another vacation somewhere else. It's like an ATM card. You just withdraw from your account the amount needed and keep the rest until next time. Now how easy is that? Another example would be: You have set aside $10,000.00 over the past year to travel. You take your first vacation and it costs you $2,000.00. You have $8,000.00 left in your vacation account to travel again somewhere. When your account is empty, your vacations are over. But next year you would have to do it all over again.

With points, you pay for your points only once and you travel forever. That's right, you get the same amount of points each "anniversary year" (the date you receive your points) forever, but you only pay for them one time. If you have a lease program, this will go on until your lease is up. If you have a deeded ownership you travel until you pass it on to the next generation and they do the same. You own it outright; it's not a lease with the "right-to-use" program. It's just that easy. You pay with your points and stay at your resorts, you exchange with your points and pay a small exchange fee either to other resorts in your program or with the exchange company your ownership is contracted to. Or exchange with other vacation options as discussed earlier. In the end, that is all there is to the points program. You can travel anywhere any other owner can but you have the added benefit of flexibility. You only need to stay a day or two instead of a week so you have full value for your ownership. You will not lose any unused portion of a fixed/floating week. And many companies permit you to roll over your points to the following year to take an extended vacation every other year if you wish. Can you see why I am a partial to the points program?

Each company/developer has additional benefits to offer so please ask what they are and why their benefits are better than their competitors.

With over 5600 resorts you have the opportunity to stay in the finest accommodations worldwide. As we previously discussed in Chapter Three, you have the benefit of the T-R-A-V-E-L-E-R expertise that was once reserved for only the very wealthy. While we were forced to sleep next to "America's Most Wanted," the wealthy traveled and stayed where we only dreamed of going. Now, the whole world is open to everyone who makes the choice to become an owner. Why wouldn't you? Have you decided the benefits outweigh the costs?

(And the costs are going to be paid anyway by paying rent at hotels as we mentioned before). Thus the question: "If I can show you a way that you can stay in the finest accommodations worldwide, in the safest locations, with all the benefits of home and costing the same money as you are spending now, would you do it?" If I can prove this to you, show you how to write it off like your home, hand you a deed to leave to generations to travel and vacation as you did, and write off every vacation you ever go on, would you be interested? And that means every vacation you take worldwide. You are only limited by your time and adventuring spirit. Go worldwide and experience all life has to offer. Travel to places others can only dream of and bring those experiences back with you. Now you can see "how the other half lives" without breaking your bank account. Imagine traveling to Italy for $219.00 for a week in a resort villa. That's right . . . $31.00 per day! WOW.

As you will find each timeshare is sold with seasons in mind. Obviously, the more popular seasons will be more expensive than off-season. Which do you think would be more expensive, a week in Vail, Colorado during ski season or after the snow melts . . . the mud season? Of course, the prime season would cost more. And whether you have a fixed/floating/points program you will pay more on the prime seasons at worldwide locations. The example would be the Red, White and Blue seasons of RCI. The red is the prime time, followed by the white season, and the blue season is "off" season. If you like to travel with the crowds then you will love the red, prime seasons. If you enjoy traveling during quieter times of the year in less crowded locations then the white and especially blue season is for you. The example of Vail would be Red during the height of the ski season. However, Vail is still a beautiful place to visit even during the summer months. If you love the mountains, you'll love Vail "off-season". You see, it all depends on how you want to travel. Again, you have total control. This is another reason why I lean to points. If you pay for a red week and you exchange to a white or blue week, you just stepped down and paid for more than you needed. If you own a white or blue week, it is almost impossible to exchange for a red week because other red week owners are trying to get there first. Who is going to accept a less expensive trade for their prime trade? When you exchange it is like-for-like, size-for-size and season-for-season. With points, you only use what you need to exchange, no more . . . no less. As we mentioned earlier, you have 122 days off each year, how do you use your traditional timeshare over the weekends? Now you have total control of what, when, where and how.

She works hard for the money, so hard for it, honey. She works hard for the money so you better treat her right. ~ Donna Summer

You work **FIFTY TO FIFTY ONE WEEKS** a year, each and every year of your life! You have ***earned the right*** to vacation for 1 to 2 weeks a year in the finest places around the world. ~ Keith G Saire, CHA

CHAPTER FIVE

"V" IS FOR VALUE

By and large, mothers and housewives are the only
workers who do not have regular time off. They
are the great vacationless class. ~Anne Morrow
Lindbergh

The value of Vacation Ownership is clear to the 4+ million owners worldwide. However, only you can decide if it is right for you. Let's go just a little deeper into the value of Vacation Ownership and look at the concept of "same money anyway." Let's say you are already spending one week per year, $200.00 per night, vacationing for 30 years. Doing the math . . . $200.00 x 7 nights = $1400.00 x 30 years = $42,000.00 total. That's $42,000.00 dollars without inflation! Just one week each year. That does not include weekend getaways or any other vacation time. Now let's continue with the assumption . . . You decide to own a timeshare. Your timeshare ownership costs you $10,000.00 with yearly maintenance fees of $500.00. $500.00 (assuming the fees remain constant) x 30 years of vacation = $15,000.00 in total maintenance fees. Add this to the upfront purchase of the timeshare of $10,000.00 and your new total is $25,000.00 before inflation. So, the original $42,000.00 in lifetime hotel rent—$25,000.00 total costs of the deed equals $17,000.00 in savings.

What would you do with an extra $17,000.00? Take the $17,000.00 savings and invest at a savings rate of 6% for 30 years. With a federal tax of 25%, a state tax of 6.8% and an inflation rate of 3%, you bank $23,362 dollars. Now, let's review: You spend $25,000.00 instead of $42,000.00 for a lifetime of vacations. Invest the difference and bank $23,362.00. That amount more than replaces the total cost of your ownership. Now that is an investment, not necessarily financial, but in your vacation future. With savings like this and a deed instead of a receipt, you tell me what makes more sense.

Want one more example? Ok, here it goes. Keep in mind timeshare should not be sold to you as an investment . . . but . . . (he says with a whisper) let me show you what I do and why I rent my timeshare. I use the formula Revenue divided by Cost. Here's how it works. Let's assume your monthly payment to own your timeshare is $250.00 per month or $3000.00 per year, your maintenance fee is $600.00 per year, add $150.00 for incidentals and another $59.00 for a Gift Certificate to put your week in the name of a "guest." To carry the thought, your guest planned on renting a hotel for $250.00 per night for one week totaling $1750.00 per week. Now let's look at the numbers: 3000 + 600 + 150 + 59 = $3809.00 per year total. This is your cost! You rent your timeshare for exactly what your "guest" is paying for the hotel room per week ($1750.00). This is your revenue. Following the formula: Revenue divided by Cost . . . $1750.00 divided by $3809.00 = .46. That is a 46% return on your timeshare "investment." If you can get that kind of return anywhere else, I want your program!

The following is a diagram that basically explains the hospitality industry. Follow along with the diagram and you will understand the hospitality industry in about five minutes.

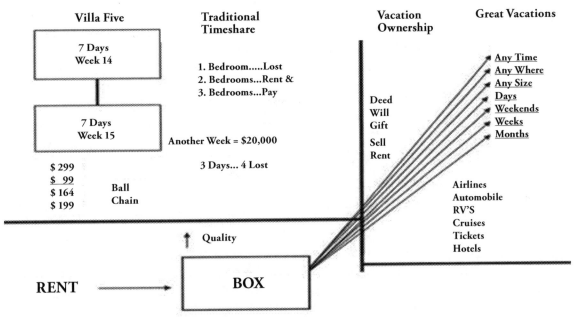

Hotel Room vs. Villa

Receipts
Memories (of the crowded room)
Bars of Soap

100%
Financial Loss

Benefits of Owning Versus Renting

OWNING

1. Hedge against inflation
2. Paying for tomorrow's vacations with today's dollars
3. Build Equity with pride of ownership with a deed and title
4. Enjoy true freedom of travel along with Tax Benefits
5. Willable with your estate
6. Opportunity to vacation in higher-quality Gold Crown Resorts and accommodations with recreational amenities
7. Positive impact on personal and family lives and a lifetime of vacation experiences

RENTING

1. Freedom of Travel
2. Receipts

The diagram is divided into three sections: Hotels on the Bottom Left, Traditional Timeshare (Fixed and Floating Weeks) on the top left and Points Ownership on the top right.

Every time we stay in a hotel we stay in a "concrete box." It's about 350 square feet (give or take). It has a bed or two with a nightstand or two, something with a television on it. If you're lucky and you've upgraded the room, there's a table and four chairs, a closet and a bathroom. That's about it. You are leaving your beautiful home or apartment and paying big money in rent to stay in your bedroom from home. Heck, you could have stayed at home and saved the money. And if it rains, where do you go? What do you do? You sit at a table in uncomfortable chairs or you are forced to sit in bed and watch one television. And what if you are traveling with children? Maybe you want to watch a sporting event or a movie and the kids want to watch cartoons. With only one TV, who wins? And the loser does what?

And every time we stay in a hotel we pay rent, don't we? Every vacation comes with a receipt, memories (of the hotel room with take-out plates and luggage spread all over), and the little bars of soap and shampoos we all take home. Financially it is a 100% loss, isn't it? Let's try to put this in perspective. If you consider your transportation, accommodations, meals and activities, how much do you spend total over the entire year, including weekend get-aways? Let's assume you spend a total of $2,000.00. That's $166.67 per month. What you don't need is another bill in your life. But timeshare is about redistributing the same money, the "anyway" money, into a deed instead of a receipt.

On the top left we find Traditional Timeshare. Fixed and floating weeks have been around since the early 1960's. But we don't travel like we did 40+ years ago. Looking at the example on the top left, let's assume you purchased a three-bedroom timeshare in Daytona Beach, Florida. You purchased a week in Villa Five and were assigned Week Fourteen (the second week of April). If you have a fixed week timeshare you would have to go to Daytona Beach every year on the second week of April and stay in your three-bedroom for one week. If you own a floating week, you can go to Daytona Beach anytime of the year, (your week floats), but you still have to stay a week at a time. And if you want to stay two weeks in a row, you would have to buy a second week wouldn't you? Now after five or six years maybe you're tired of going to Daytona Beach. The only way to go somewhere else is to join an exchange company. Here you decided to join RCI. At the time of this printing RCI is $295 to join and $99 each year in dues just to have them mail their resort catalog and the "Endless Vacation" magazine every other month. If you want to travel anywhere within the United States, Canada or Hawaii, you pay the exchange fee which is currently $164.00. If you want to travel internationally, the exchange fee as of this writing is $199.00.

How does this work? Again, you own a three-bedroom. You want to exchange to a resort on the black sand beach in Hawaii. You give RCI your week to exchange for a resort in Hawaii, so they have your week before you know what you get in return. After you "bank" your week, RCI calls you back and tells you "we have good news and a little bad news. We found accommodations in Hawaii but they only have a one bedroom, is that OK with you?" You are forced to step down and pay more for something less than you own. And what if you planned to travel with friends or family and you **NEED** a three bedroom? Oh well! So you have to take it if you want to go. Now, if you own a three bedroom in Daytona Beach and you are forced to take a one bedroom in Hawaii, what happened to the other two bedrooms you paid for? That's right, you lost them. And the two bedrooms you are not using in Daytona! What is the company doing with them? That's right, they're renting them out. But do they give you the rent? No? So, you paid for it, you pay maintenance fees to maintain it and they are renting out your ownership and keeping the money! What is wrong with that picture?

And as we said earlier, if you want more than a week vacation each year, you need to spend more money to buy an entire second week. But what if you want to get away for a three-day weekend? You go for three days but you own an entire week. What happened to the other four days of that week? That's right, you lose them!

Now, looking at your timeshare chart on the top left of Page 22 let's recap traditional timeshare. You own a three-bedroom villa in Daytona Beach and after five years you decide to exchange. You bank your week with RCI and pay the exchange fees. If they have your accommodations, that's great. If not, you lose and lose and lose. Who is controlling your vacation more, you or the traditional timeshare? By now, I'm sure you'll agree it is traditional timeshare. That is why developers are now offering points programs. They finally began to listen to consumers, who were told they would have great vacations when staying in resorts. "Look at all the amenities a resort can offer that hotels cannot." They had a ball when they stayed at a resort; but it was a ball-and-chain vacation if they had to go to the same place year after year with very limited flexibility. They could exchange with exchange companies, pay the exchange fees and take what is offered whether or not it fit their needs. But if not, they were forced to lose, and lose, and lose, and lose across the board.

On the top right you will find the Points Program. When asked by developers how to make timeshare better the owners said they want to go **ANY TIME, ANYWHERE, use ANY SIZE they needed when they needed it.** Maybe you want to go for a day or two. Can you use a fixed or floating week for that? Maybe you want to get away for a three-day weekend. Can you use a traditional timeshare for that? Well, I guess you can if you don't mind losing the other four days of the week, but then what are you paying for? Maybe you want to go a week, or two, or three, or maybe you want to go a month or more. The only way to do that with a traditional timeshare is to have four deeds, four property taxes, and four maintenance fees. You have four of everything. To me personally, that makes no sense at all. I challenge anyone to explain to me how owning traditional timeshare makes sense financially.

What does make sense is to own rather than rent a hotel room. Without a deed, you will rent for the rest of your life. You will not be able to will it to someone. Without a deed you cannot give it to someone. Without a deed, you have nothing to sell should you decide someday to sell it. And if you have more vacation time available to you through your ownership, why not rent it out like the developer does with your traditional timeshare? Put the money back in your pocket. How do you do all of that with receipts in a shoebox? (Please note: Timeshare is not to be used as an investment; it is about vacations. However, what you do with your deed after you own it is entirely up to you. If you were not able to rent it, the developers, timeshare rental internet sites and so on, would not be able to rent it either. At least rent it on your own and keep all the money or let someone rent it for you and pay a small commission. Why let your ownership go to waste? Put some money back in your pocket if you are unable to use it as you wish).

If we just stop right here, knowing what you know now, what makes more sense to you . . . staying in a hotel and paying rent, owning a traditional timeshare with the limitations of a fixed or floating week or owning a points program? You can probably tell I lean to the points program (but I did tell you that before).

Here is another example of "Rent VS. Own". A much simpler version:

In 2008 you decide to purchase a timeshare with the "anyway" money you spend in hotels to get a deed instead of a receipt. Now let's go to an extreme example to show you the impact of what this ownership means. From the day you become an owner to thirty years later, let's say there is no such thing as "equity" in the United States. The value of property never goes up, not one cent in thirty years (I told you this was an extreme).

You bought it for $20,000 . . . you used it for thirty years and you were forced to sell thirty years later for $20,000.00. How much did it cost you to travel for thirty years?

2008   2038

$20,000.00 $20,000.00

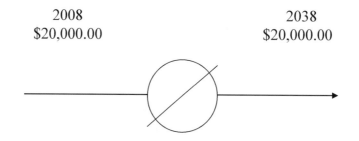

<u>Your right, NOTHING!</u> Now let's take it to one more extreme because I hear you saying "but what about all the maintenance and exchange fees I had to pay. It wasn't free"! Fair enough. Here is my response. Let's say you were forced to sell it for HALF of what you paid. You bought it for $20,000 and sold it for $10,000. You lost half your money. Now that is a lousy investment for the future, even in my book. Except . . . if you keep the $20,000.00 worth of receipts in a shoebox and thirty years from now you tried to sell them, what are you going to get? Exactly, nothing, zero, zilch. It is nothing but pieces of paper in a box. So which is better for you now? And keep in mind, if after thirty years, if you just stay one more day in a hotel . . . it starts all over again. Now what makes more sense to you?

Consider also that accommodations are not your only vacations expenses. You also have expenses for AIRLINES, AUTOMOBILE RENTAL, RECREATIONAL VEHICLES, CRUISES, ENTERTAINMENT, TICKETS and yes, even HOTELS. Many developers of points-based timeshare have now joined with other service providers to offer the additional amenities that neither hotels nor traditional timeshare can offer. You pay for your points once and are able to use them however you see fit. Not a bad investment in your future.

When you rent you have freedom of travel and a box of receipts. When you own a timeshare you have a hedge against inflation, you are paying for tomorrow's vacations with today's dollars, you build equity with the pride of owning a deed and title, you will enjoy <u>true freedom of travel</u> along with **huge tax benefits.** Your ownership is willable with your estate or trust; you have the opportunity to vacation in higher-quality Gold Crown or Five Star Resorts and accommodations with recreational amenities. And most of all, there will be a positive impact on your personal and family lives and a lifetime of vacation experiences with direct impact on health and well-being.

Consider the value of vacations as a medical savings. What better value than your wellness? Life, friends and family, bills, your job and other uncontrollable forces add stress and tension to our lives. This stress takes its toll daily. Sometimes you can feel the heaviness of the world on your shoulders. Sometimes you just feel like hiding in your closet, away from everything for a while just to rest and relax. This is stress! This is why you need a vacation. I see it this way. When using a computer over time, more and more information gets stored on the hard drive. You need to do a disk cleanup and sometimes a disk defragmentation to clear the "junk" off the hard drive. If not, your drive runs slower and slower until it finally crashes. Our brain is nothing but the world's best computer system running 24/7/365. It never rests. If we don't clear the "hard drive" every now and then, it begins to slow down. If we don't listen to the signs, anything can happen. Stress disorders, tension headaches, stress-related illnesses, and if you don't listen then . . . worse. Your body will do what it needs to do to survive. It will slow down just to keep moving, to avoid crashing like a computer hard drive. This is the reason we **MUST** have vacations. We must get away. We must rest our bodies and our minds or our bodies will do it for us. According to Alan Muney, MD, executive vice president and chief medical officer at Oxford Health Plans, Inc., "We need to take vacations seriously. While we readily accept that getting immunizations, taking vitamins, or getting mammograms and pap smears is good preventive medicine, something as simple as taking a vacation is not accepted." In the September-October 2000 edition of the medical journal "Psychosomatic Medicine" a study was done proving that vacationing could prevent heart disease. Cardiologist Stephen Sinatra, assistant clinical professor of medicine at the University of Connecticut School of Medicine in Farmington, when told that his patients couldn't afford a vacation, said, "they can't afford not to take one." And both doctors agree on one thing. A three-day weekend is not enough. Dr. Muney told WebMD "A lot of what this is all about is a mental attitude. When you come back, you should feel refreshed with a new perspective." He recommends employers monitor those employees that work too much.

<u>Fitness Magazine, July 2007</u> had a small but significant article in the Health Section. It was titled "Must. Take. Vacation. Now." It states most Americans get an average of 14 days annually yet we give up about four of them every year. They offer three reasons why you need to vacation.

Your heart . . . "Time off can cut your risk of a heart attack by almost 800 percent (imagine . . . 800 percent!), according to the Farmingham Heart Study. The findings confirmed the benefit for both working women and stay-at-home moms. Those who went away at least twice a year were the least likely to suffer a heart attack." 2. Your family. "A survey by the Families and Work Institute shows that many women feel overworked and overwhelmed. And the tension trickles down: Thirty-four percent of kids polled said they wished their mothers were less stressed and tired." 3. Your happiness. "Women who take two or more trips a year have happier marriages and are less likely to suffer from depression, reports the Wisconsin Rural Women's Health Study."

And one more if you don't believe. Dr. Brooks Gump of the Department of Psychology at the State University of New York at Oswego conducted a study over a nine-year period on 12,000 men at high risk for heart disease. The results showed that men taking vacations had significantly less risk of dying from heart disease, or for that matter, any other condition than men who didn't take vacation. Remember, the world was created in six days with one day to rest. Vacations are your time to rest. And your wellness will improve. Your wellness depends on it.

Also, how would you like a pay increase? Vacations may be able to do this for you also. Here's why. You work day after day, plodding along on your job, working to your peak day after day. You accomplish everything your boss asks you to do. About six months into the year you begin to slow down a bit. You still do everything to expectations but it seems to take a little longer to do it. You find you might need to stay over after the workday to finish. After about nine months, you are really stressed. You hate Mondays. You can't wait for Friday to arrive. On Wednesday you are still looking at two more days but at least you are over the hump. By now you find that your job performance is suffering and you find it harder and harder to get up and go into work everyday. Your body is talking to you. Are you listening? It needs a rest. Your boss starts wondering why you are not producing like you once did. You're "looking tired." Even co-workers begin to notice. Finally, finally your boss suggests some time off. And wisely you decide to listen. You take a vacation and rejuvenate yourself. You come back tanned, rested and ready to get back to whatever life throws at you. Your boss notices your newly acquired exuberance and performance. It has been a year since your last evaluation. Your boss tells you how pleased he is with your performance and what a great future you have with the company, offering a pay increase for your due-diligence and abilities. You rested, you listened and you were rewarded. Perhaps the next evaluation will bring a promotion and another pay increase. And by resting you have saved on medical insurance claims, doctor bills, hospital costs and lost work time due to illness. You see, vacations do make you more successful and wealthier. Please keep in mind, when someone is on their death bed surrounded by their family, they never look up and say, "I'm sorry I didn't work one more day." They say, "I wish we had a little more time together." And their family would give everything they have, every thing they own for just one more week, just one more day with their loved one. Wouldn't they! **Wouldn't you?**

As a timeshare owner you may have the opportunity to rent out your ownership if you chose not to use it. To be safe, please check with your developer to see if you are permitted to do so. Let me add this caveat: Timeshare ownership has nothing to do with investing. It's about vacation, but what you do with your ownership is up to you as long as you are permitted by your deed.

Let's assume you're not able to use your timeshare completely this year. You own two weeks but can only travel one week this year. What are you going to do with the extra week? Of course you can let your family members use it, you can donate it to a non-profit and write it off for the tax advantage or you can rent it out and put the money back in your pocket to offset the costs of ownership. There are many ways to rent your timeshare. The best is word of mouth. Your friends are going to take a vacation so instead of them renting a hotel, you let them pay you the same and upgrade to a villa instead of a hotel room. Plus you saved them a small fortune in restaurant costs. You can find renters on Ebay, Timeshare Rentals, Red Week or other places and companies. Your developer may have a rental option for you also. Check with them.

There are numerous ways to find renters. Permit me to show you a more off-the-wall way of doing it. I find less competition and more success this way. First, I need to plan on where I want to rent a resort. I can either rent my own resort or through the exchange companies and make my friends my "guest." I then go to the Internet or make calls and get a copy of the calendar of events for the areas I am interested in. Let's use Daytona Beach again for our example. Ask yourself, "When is the best time to rent a resort in Daytona Beach"? You aren't sure so you go to the Visitors Bureau and get a copy of their "Calendar of Events." You find the dates for the Daytona 500, Bike Week (when almost 500,000 riders roll in every year), spring and fall breaks and others. When all the hotels are completely sold out for speed week and bike week, do you think you can ask a premium price for your resort? If hotels are asking and getting $300-$400 per night, what will you get for your fully equipped resort? At the very least you match the hotels for $2100-$2800 per week. If your monthly payment is $200 per month, your timeshare will cost you out-of-pocket for the year $300 at the low end or you can bank $400 and have the year paid off for you. Does this sound like a reasonable return on your vacation investment? Consider Myrtle Beach, South Carolina for the summer; Gatlinburg, Tennessee when the leaves change in the mountains; Branson, Missouri at Christmas; Orlando, Florida anytime and don't forget Daytona Beach. You can do this anywhere if you do a little research and successfully ask and receive premium rental income. After all, the hotels ask and get it. And as a side note, let me help you further with this little known tax loophole. If you rent anything for fourteen days or less, the rental income is tax exempt. If you rent for fifteen days or more, you are obligated to pay taxes on the rental income. If you rent two weeks that's fourteen days. Your $2800 per week is now $5600 tax-free! Not a bad value for your vacation investment.

Hotels. Hotels are great because you can find one in almost any town. The door is always open and you are always welcome. There are so many types to fit every budget. You can stay nightly or you can have an extended stay. They are great for the visiting family, vacationing family or the traveling businessman or businesswoman. Unfortunately, they also offer the same for "Americas Most Wanted." When you stay in a timeshare, you are traveling with the elite of our times, part of a moving community. For that brief period, they are your new neighbors. You have a unique opportunity to visit your neighbors, share a soda, visit the pool, play tennis, enjoy a round of golf and make new friends from all over the world. Timeshare owners are from every walk of life, from different age groups, cultures, and beliefs. It provides us the unique opportunity to learn daily from guests who are "one of us." Hotels are great, but give me the opportunity to meet someone around the pool at a resort over the pool at a hotel anytime. You are home and always welcome. Rent VS. Own.

Here is a little known idea that was given to me by a pastor of a church. Now, I don't want to get into the whole games-of-chance-in-church debate. If you and your church don't believe in games of chance I don't wish to offend. Simply replace the church with a youth group, the PTA, the Boy or Girl Scouts, the high school band or any other organization that needs to raise money to support their cause. Here is how it was explained to me: The church sells numbered tickets that match the state lottery. Obviously, they sell 1000 tickets. They sell each ticket for $50.00. I know, that's a lot of money for a ticket, but wait until you hear the prize: a one-week vacation for a family of four to anywhere in the world, all expenses paid. Imagine a family of four taking a one-week vacation for $50.00! Anyway, the pastor said the community couldn't wait for this ticket to come out. People want it to be offered twice a year. The church is expanding and they need to build an addition that offers a school to the children. Here is what he told me. The pastor said, "Keith, we sell 1000 tickets at $50.00 each. That means we make $50,000 on the sale of these tickets. But let's break down the costs. If we purchase airline tickets far enough in advance, how much do you think we pay . . . $1000 per ticket? Ok, four tickets are $4000. If we rent a car for one week far enough in advance how much will that cost, about $500? And we promised "all expenses paid," so we give each one $1000 in spending cash to do whatever he or she wants. And if they go anywhere they choose, it will cost $199.00 for accommodations, because that is the current exchange fee for RCI to travel internationally. So let's break that down:

Airline Tickets	$ 4000
Cash for each member	$ 4000
Automobile Rental	$ 500
Timeshare Exchange Fee	$ 199
Total cost to Church	$ 8699
Total Net to Church	$ 41301

The pastor said, "Keith, even if it costs us $10,000 we still put $40,000 into our building fund." That's not a bad return. Now that's real value! And keep in mind; any organization can do the same. Our youth will no longer need to sell magazines, candy and fudge door-to-door. We don't know who's behind those doors any more. That's why parents usually buy everything their children sell so the kids won't have to go knocking on the doors of strangers. I just thought I would pass this along in case anyone can use the information.

I believe the single most valuable benefit of owning a timeshare is the legacy we leave behind. With timeshare, we have the opportunity throughout our lifetime to share special time with friends and family, building memories that last forever. As children, we travel with our family and build precious memories. As we grow older, we reflect on those memories. Someday, in the cycle of life, everyone is forced to leave this earth. Our friends and family will reflect on the time together, smile at the good times shared and find that warm spot in their hearts. There is an old saying . . . "no one is ever gone as long as they live within the hearts and minds of others!" This is part of the legacy. Those left behind count on this legacy and continue to appreciate this legacy with their own friends and family. Thus, the cycle of life.

Part of the legacy is the ability to leave this opportunity to others. My brother, Kevin, traveled with our parents and grandparents when we were little. My brother passed when he was a young man in his thirties, yet he lives on in our hearts and thoughts. He left that legacy behind.

Part of my legacy is the time spent with our daughter, Carrie. We reflect back on the places we visited and the experiences we shared. We now have grandchildren, Alison, Lauren and Jacob. Part of our legacy is to share with them some of the experiences we shared with Carrie. They, in turn, share their excitement, joy and youth, keeping us young at heart. I will reflect on those memories; that is my legacy.

Carrie lost her husband, Rick, to brain cancer about two weeks before Christmas, 2006. It was a difficult time for the family, but it was the memories, the legacy, that pulled everyone together and gave them strength to carry on. Now Carrie is able to travel with her children, building memories as they did with their father. That is Rick's legacy. If they only had one more week, just one more day! Timeshare has the innate power to do that in everyone's life. It is the legacy that continues to give forever. Ama Credi E Vai.

We joke that we will always be remembered at least one time a year, when our grandchildren take their children where we once took them on vacation. They will open the door to a resort villa somewhere in the world and have to say "thanks pap and gram," because we left that legacy behind. Our homes will be sold, our bank account used, our cars will be gone, but, in the end, our legacy of vacation continues. When was the last time you heard someone on their deathbed say, "I wish I could have spent one more day at work?" Start building your legacy.

CHAPTER SIX

"E" IS FOR EXCHANGE

> The World is a book, and those who do not travel read only a page. ~St. Augustine

We went into the exchange companies in some depth earlier in Chapter Three. I won't make you suffer through that again by repeating all the information. Let us recap some of the basic information.

The two largest exchange companies are RCI and Interval International. RCI has about 3800 resorts in their system and II has about 1800 resorts with them. There are a few other players in the exchange field such as Hawaii Timeshare Exchange, Platinum Exchange and so on.

With fixed and floating ownerships, you must look at demand area, location for location, quality for quality, size for size, and season for season. You must consider WHAT and WHERE you own to benefit fully from your ownership. If not, you may be forced to step down and accept less than what you paid for. This is my most important point. You may be forced to pay much more than comfortably affordable to benefit fully from your ownership. Owning is not supposed to hurt; it's supposed to heal. As one of my wise friends taught me "Ownership is to be a blessing, not a stressing!" Let's look at this in detail.

Demand Area: You may have heard the term "trading power." If you have a resort in a high demand area it will be much easier to trade. You will travel to other high demand areas because you can offer your high-demand area for trade. You can also step down to a lesser demand area because you have the power of trade on your side. However, you are forced to accept less. My question is always "If I pay for the best to have the best, and I'm forced to step down to less than best as a demand area, what am I paying for?" But this is what you must do in traditional timeshare to travel to where you want. This ties in the location-for-location trade. Where do you want to go and when do you want to be there?

Quality-for Quality: This again depends on what you have to offer in trade. With RCI you have Gold Crown resorts and with II you have Five-Star resorts. The American Resort Developers Association (ARDA) sets these independent ratings, which are not unlike AAA ratings for hotels. Very particular guidelines must be met to earn these ratings. Gold Crown and Five-Star resorts offer the best quality. With these you have the ability to trade for any resort you wish. Again, you may be forced to accept a lesser quality resort to travel to a particular destination. Therefore, if you are willing, and can afford to spend the money, you want to own the best-rated resort in the best demand area. The best rating means you can always trade for a "like" resort. If you own a lesser quality resort you may not be able to trade up, but you will always be able to trade Quality-for-Quality or less. So again I ask, "If you own the best and are forced to accept less, what are you paying for?"

Size-for-Size: The more occupancy your villa provides the better the trade. The size of the unit is usually based on the number it will sleep. So, if you own a villa that will sleep a total of twelve (usually a three-bedroom), you will not be able to trade up to a four-bedroom villa or cabin. You will always be able to trade down to a one or two-bedroom villa that sleeps fewer total quests but you must trade size-for-size or lose. So the best trading power is for the largest available. If you cannot afford the best, you must settle for less. And if you can and you are forced to step down to travel where you want to go, you are forced to lose. You are caught between the rock-and-hard-place. Either way, I think you lose.

Season-for-Season: Both RCI and II use color codes to decide what season you are traveling. This color code determines the demand of the resorts. With RCI they are Red, White and Blue. With II they are Red, Yellow and Green. Red is the best. This is the high-demand season for the resort. This would be Vail, Colorado during the prime ski season. Then you have the White or Yellow season which is a medium-demand season, also called the shoulder. This is when demand is beginning to wind down. And then there is Blue or Green season. This is the off-season. This is after the snow melts in Vail. Vail is still a beautiful place to travel during the "mud" season; you just need another reason for going other than skiing.

To recap the seasons, the following are the color codes at a glance:

Season	RCI	Interval International
High Season	Red	Red
Medium Season	White	Yellow
Low Season	Blue	Green

To be able to travel anytime, anywhere you will need to own a Red week. Again, you trade for what you own. You control your vacations. If you want to travel off-peak season, you are forced to step down your ownership. You can always trade down but you may not be able to trade up. One more time . . . "If you are paying for the best and you are forced to accept less, you lose. What are you paying for?" This all goes back to our Rent Vs Own chart as a recap.

You are the only one able to decide what you own and what you can afford. Please, do your homework before signing anything. Ask the questions and "Buyer Beware."

This is one of the largest reasons I lean so strongly to the points program. With a pure points program you control your travel experience. Go back and look at the Rent—Vs—Own chart and you will understand. You decide where, when and what size when you need it. You will never be forced to overpay again. And with a "pure-points program" you will also gain one more freedom. With the traditional timeshare program you own an exchange program. With a pure-points program you have a reservations program. You see, for an exchange program to work, someone that owns where you want to stay must first exchange somewhere else. If they choose to stay and use their resort, you cannot exchange to it. They are using it! All you will ever hear then is "sorry, there is no availability." And if you do get the chance to stay at the resort you will have to check-in/ check-out on either Friday-Friday, Saturday-Saturday or Sunday-Sunday. With a pure-points program you can travel daily if you wish. You can check-in on what day you want and check-out when you want. As an example, you can check-in at an Orlando, Florida resort on a Monday and check-out on a Wednesday and then go to Daytona Beach for a few days if you want. You are never trapped at a specific location for a week at a time. Because it is a reservation program, you just book your vacation resort either by phone or online (personally, I like online) like a hotel but you pay with your points. Of course, everything is based on availability, but when everyone is traveling at different times you have more openings to schedule when you want. Think about it, if hotels could only rent their rooms by the week, would they make money? And would you stay there if you had to pay for a week and leave in three days? Of course not! Everyone loses. With the reservation program, everyone wins.

As a side note: How about an additional savings? When you are forced to travel only on weekends, you pay top money to fly. You save extensively on flights if you fly on weekdays and cut your travel expenses.

Let's look briefly at one resort points exchange program with RCI.

Points-to-Week for RCI Exchange

STUDIO

Blue Week	=	3000 Points
White Week	=	4000 Points
Red Week	=	5000 Points

ONE BEDROOM

Blue Week	=	4000 Points
White Week	=	5000 Points
Red Week	=	6000 Points

TWO BEDROOM

Blue Week	=	6000 Points
White Week	=	8000 Points
Red Week	=	10000 Points

This is **not** a "Pure-Points" program. This is an internal exchange points program with a weeks exchange. This means when you want to travel between resorts within the same developer you have points. But if you want to exchange outside the developers resorts (with RCI or II) you need to convert your points to weeks. With pure-points, there is no conversion necessary. Just use your points.

Now let's look at an example of a Points-to-Week Conversion for resorts without pure points. As you can see by this Points-to-Week Conversion chart, you only pay for what you need. Let's say you want to travel to a resort and stay in a one-bedroom during a Red week. With this chart you would need to exchange 6000 points to get exactly what you want. You will not pay 10,000 points for a two-bedroom when you only need a one bedroom. If you wish to trade up because you need a two-bedroom, you only need to spend an additional 4000 points to acquire what you need. You will not use 10,000 points and step down to a one-bedroom that should only be 6000 points. Again, only pay for what you need, when you need it. Decide where you want to go, find the resort where you wish to stay, locate the season you are traveling and use your points to pay for only what you need. You are back in control! The obvious follows. Only pay for what you need and what you can afford at the time. You choose the demand time you wish to travel, quality for quality, size for size and season for season. You can always buy more points at a later time if you want to upgrade your ownership. The developer will always be more than willing to take more of your money (jokingly). And of course, you will need to pay the fee to the exchange company. You now have more than 5600 resorts from which to choose.

There is an old saying in the Timeshare Industry. "Land doesn't trade for sand." This holds true for fixed and floating week ownership. Let's say you own a resort in the Pocono Mountains in Pennsylvania. You decide you want to travel to the Caribbean to your dream island. You need to exchange. Ask yourself, "Do the owners of the resort in the Caribbean want to travel to the Pocono Mountains when they exchange?" This is all about trading power. If you own a resort in Orlando, Florida you may have more of a chance because it is all based on where the island owners want to go. Do they want to go to the Pocono's or Orlando? Where do you think you have more trading power? This is a simplistic example but you get the idea. If you have points, you can exchange from any resort in your developer's offerings and offer your island partner exactly what he wants. In the end . . . it is all about flexibility. Do you need it, want it and will you use it? If you answer yes, you need points. If not, you need fixed or floating weeks. In real estate the number one rule is location, location, location . . . yes, especially with a fixed or floating week ownership but not with points. It doesn't matter where you own. Just use your points and travel the way you were meant to. It is a little like the stock market. With a "Pure-Points" program (such as RCI Points), I always suggest my owners "buy low and trade high." With pure points you can pay for your points at an inexpensive resort, a resort you have no intention of staying and trade up to a better resort in the area.

Here is an example of buying, owning and trading with RCI Points. You can buy your points at a Three-Star (RCI Hospitality rated) and the same points will trade into a Gold Crown Resort. Become an owner at a lesser-rated resort (buy low) and stay at the best resort offered with the same points program (trade high). You see, just like the stock market, buy low and sell high.

Let's summarize some of the information above. When you become an owner, unless you are buying a fixed week to travel to the same resort each year, buy with exchanging in mind. And in doing so, keep in mind the rules of exchange. If you want to exchange into popular destinations you need a popular destination to exchange with or you may run into the difficulties we just explained. Even with a points program you will need to plan ahead and be flexible. However, with a "pure points" program like the RCI Points Program, this is less of a concern. You must be willing to trade down with traditional timeshare. Not necessarily with a points program. In fact, you have a better chance of trading up based on availability.

CHAPTER SEVEN

"L" IS FOR LUXURY

> Isn't it interesting that people feel best about themselves right before they go on vacation? They've cleared up all of their to-do piles, closed up transactions, and renewed old promises with themselves. My most basic suggestion is that people should do that more than once a year.
> ~ David Allen

As with hotels, resorts have various levels of luxury. These can be found through the ratings provided by ARDA and the guidelines set by each exchange company. Let's briefly touch on the luxury of the Five-Star and Gold Crown Resorts.

Gold Crown and Five-Star resorts are the highest level of excellence in affiliated resort accommodations and hospitality. Affiliated resorts have met exacting quality and service standards based on both Subscribing Members Comment Card ratings and an ARDA evaluation of resort facilities, amenities and services.

When you walk through the doors of a resort villa you are looking and expecting what RCI calls the "Ahhhh" factor. You know you are home-away-from-home. When you walk through the doors you take a moment to look around and begin to relax knowing you are ""home." When you stay in hotels, even the finest hotels, you are still paying to stay in your bedroom at home. Granted, their bedroom may be a bit more over the top than ours at home but isn't that what we pay for? To be wowed! But in the end, it is still a concrete box and nothing more than a bedroom with a television, maybe a table four chairs, a closet and a bathroom. And if you normally stay in studio hotels, you may have a separate sitting area from the bedroom, but that's about it. Can you really tell me a hotel room or studio is better than a resort villa? And if it were the same amount of money you're going to spend anyway, where would you like to stay? And frankly, even if it is a little bit more, isn't worth it? That is something only you can decide.

The amenities make your villa into a home-away-from-home. Just take a look at what resorts offer in each villa. Of course, not all resorts have all the options but most have the resort basics. You will possibly find a partial or full kitchen with a stove, oven, microwave, full-size refrigerator, dishwasher, all the small appliances you left at home, and the entire dish; glass and silverware items you need to prepare meals and save a fortune on restaurants. The kitchen is great even if you are only looking for a quick breakfast or a nightly snack before bed. Instead of ordering a pizza that arrives cold with the cheese stuck to the lid, you reach into the freezer and bake your own pizza while you are relaxing in the whirlpool in your master bedroom. Now that's home: a whirlpool bath and a hot pizza.

And there's a washer and dryer so you only need to travel with half the luggage. You can do laundry while down at the pool or spa. One of the things I hate most is going to the pool, coming back to the room and deciding to go back to the pool, forced to tug on wet, clammy, cold, nasty swimming trunks. Now I can go to the pool, come back for lunch, throw my trunks in the dryer, take them out dry and warm, slip them on without the fight and head back to the pool.

There is a complete living room with a pullout sleeper sofa, television and stereo sound system to relax just like at home. There are televisions in every room, additional bedrooms, king-sized beds and a lock on the master bedroom door for privacy. You have all the bedding needed, and a safe to lock up your valuables. There's a vacuum cleaner for spills; why disturb your privacy with the hassles of housekeeping? I can go on and on, but you get the idea. Look around your villa and close your eyes and see your home. Not much is missing. You even have an Internet connection.

And don't forget the luxurious amenities of the resort itself. After all, you didn't travel to sit in your villa. You want to experience the offerings of the resort and surrounding area. At home you would probably have to drive for miles and miles to find what you have right at the resort. You find indoor/outdoor heated pools, children's pools, children water parks, water slides, lazy rivers, whirlpools, spas, steam rooms, saunas, beaches in your back yard, nature trails, horseback riding, golf courses, lakes for boating and fishing, miniature golf courses, bowling alleys, game rooms and children's activities. What more do you want and how much can you do here that you don't or can't do at home?

And look at the surroundings. Resorts are in the finest places around the world where people want to visit the most. Developers do ongoing surveys to find where we want to go and what we want to do when we get there. These are called "discoveries." When you visit a resort the developers will do a discovery for two reasons. One: They try to find where you want to go and what you want to do when you get there, and Two: they "discover" how you like to travel and how they can help you make it happen with their resort. Now this is luxury!

And oh, by the way, <u>National Geographic Traveler</u> got it right when it said: "Baby Boomers want to spend time with family and less time planning trips. Unlike standard hotel rooms, timeshares-often with two or three bedrooms-can accommodate children." Personally, I believe the greatest luxury is to spend quality time with family and friends in my own "condo" rather than renting two or three hotel rooms. How do you share and build the quality time when you are separated most of the time? Now you can go in and kiss the kids goodnight and later, quietly peek in and check on them to make sure they are all right, just like home.

CHAPTER EIGHT

"E" IS FOR EDUCATION

> Each vacation I visited either France or Germany to
> improve my languages…
> ~ Patrick White

Before you decide to buy a timeshare you should educate yourself to be fully informed on what you are buying and what you need. Let's take a crash course. If you are vacationing in a popular vacation/resort destination such as Orlando, Florida I promise you will run into an OPC (off-premise contact). In the timeshare sales industry these folks are fondly known as "body snatchers." Their job is to invite you to take a timeshare tour at a resort they represent. They usually offer some type of incentive to visit and listen to a ninety-minute to two-hour presentation about the timeshare and what the developer has to offer. You may find an advertisement on the Internet, a telemarketer may call on the phone or maybe you put your name in a "box" trying to win a "free vacation" called a "mini-vac" (mini vacation). Here is a little known fact, everyone wins when they drop their name in the box. The resort can only survive if they have guests or "tours" to present and sell to. No visitors, no sales. When you arrive you will check-in at a welcome desk to confirm your arrival and log you in for your incentive. Your name will then be added to a rotation list and a sales representative will be randomly chosen to show you the presentation and the resort, answer all your questions and obviously ask you to buy today. As a side note: you will feel a bit of "pressure" to buy today because of the business practice of the industry. This is not pressure per say. Chances are, the sales representative works on straight commission and if you don't become an owner, they don't pay their bills and feed the kids. Also, they must maintain a "closing ratio." They may have been put on a probation period and must close two out of the next ten guests they see. It is the nature of the business.

Please permit me to vent a bit here. This is where I strongly disagree with those taking advantage of the system. These abusers travel from resort-to-resort looking for free gifts such as theme park tickets, restaurant certificates, ski lift tickets, etc. They waste their time, those with them and the sales representative for a free "gift" that isn't really a gift anyway.

The guests must sit for hours on end with no intention of buying. It doesn't make sense to me personally. They are on vacation. Enjoy the limited time. Now please don't get me wrong here. There can be no sale without a guest and every guest is important to the resort. I'm only concerned for those that make a "career" of touring with no intention of becoming an owner anywhere. This only hurts everyone. Every tour costs the resort $200—$600 per guest, depending if the resort is paying for a "mini-vac" (accommodations, gifts, etc.). If the resort has one hundred guests per day, they are paying out $20,000—$60,000 per day, 7 days per week. Now you can see why the resort wants you to buy "today." They will even drop the price to make that happen, so ask for the "drop." If everyone is permitted to "think about it" and come back, the costs to the resort just doubled. If it were your business, how would you run your business? You must agree, you would want the sale today also. This additional cost to the resort drives the price of the resort up to do business. And of course, who ends up paying the higher costs? That's right, you and me. And don't forget, it may be the last tour the sales representative may have.

If you finance your timeshare you will probably pay higher interest rates than you can get at other financial institutions. One of the reasons for this is everyone has guaranteed financing. They don't know if someone has filed for bankruptcy or what their credit rating is at the time of the sale. They are taking all the risks so the interest rates are high. My recommendation to everyone is to only buy with no prepayment penalty. That way you can get financing on your own and pay it off soon saving you money. I always strongly suggest an owner look for an independent bi-weekly representative and set up bi-weekly payments. You pay exactly the same payment per month (plus a small fee to debit your account) and you will save about one third of your time and money. In effect you have cut your interest rate and the amount of interest payback. Every year has two months with five weeks. If you are paying bi-weekly you will make a painless additional payment per year. The payment is applied directly to your principal so you in effect get out of debt sooner because less is being financed. Let's look at this a little closer. You purchased a three bedroom every year timeshare in a great destination location for exchange possibilities. You are now converting to a Bi-Weekly Payment.

Here is the following breakdown to make an informed decision:

Mortgage	$25000.00
Interest Rate	17.5%
Mortgage Length in Months	120
Monthly Payment	$442.45
Payment with Escrow	$442.45
Bi-Weekly Payment	$221.23
Additional Payment (Bi-Weekly)	$000.00
Total Bi-Weekly Payment	$221.23

What is this savings to you by going Bi-Weekly?

Type of Payment	Years to Pay Off	Total Cost of Loan	Total Interest Paid	Total Interest Saved	Net Equivalent Int. Rate	Percent of Int. Saved
Standard	10.00	$53,086.84	$28,086.84	$000.00	17.5%	0%
Bi-Weekly	8.42	$47,625.33	$22,625.33	$5,461.51	14.10%	19.45%
Additional Bi-Weekly	8.42	$47,625.33	$22,625.33	$5,461.51	14.10%	19.45%

To recap: Your mortgage will be paid off in **8.42** years instead of **10.00**. You will have saved **$5461.51** in unnecessary interest payments! You will have reduced the amount of interest you are paying by **19.45%**.

Now let's address this example one more time but with a minor addition to the payment.

Notice the impact of what a little more can do:

Mortgage	$25000.00
Interest Rate	17.5%
Mortgage Length in Months	120
Monthly Payment	$442.45
Payment with Escrow	$442.45
Bi-Weekly Payment	$221.23
Additional Payment (Bi-Weekly)	$25.00
Total Bi-Weekly Payment	$246.23

What is the savings to you by going Bi-Weekly with a minor additional adjustment?

Type of Payment	Years to Pay Off	Total Cost of Loan	Total Interest Paid	Total Interest Saved	Net Equivalent Interest Rate	Percent of Interest Saved
Standard	10.00	$53,086.84	$28,086.84	$000.00	17.5%	0%
Bi-Weekly	8.42	$47,625.33	$22,625.33	$5,461.51	14.10%	19.45%
Additional Biweekly	6.83	$42,869.00	$17.869.00	$10,217.84	11.13%	36.38%

To Recap: Your mortgage will be paid off in **6.83** years instead of **10.00**. You will have saved **$10,217.84** in unnecessary interest payments! You will reduce the amount of interest you are paying by **36.38%.**

What will you do with a **$10,217.84** savings?

And be sure to also ask the sales representative about setting up an EFT (electronic funds transfer) to either your checking account or credit card. If you have a credit card that offers a reward program for using the card, use it and gain the additional benefit while paying off your timeshare. Ask about a resale to save money over new, additional "first-day" incentives for buying that day, additional discounts if you buy more than one week or a certain amount of points and don't forget to ask for additional benefits if you put down more than the standard 10%.

It is also recommended to ask these additional questions:

- Σ What kind of exchange power do I have if I want to exchange?
- Σ What size unit do I need, or how many points do I need?
- Σ Will I be able to upgrade later?
- Σ What amenities does the resort have and what are the additional fees if I use them?
- Σ Does the resort belong to ARDA (American Resort Development Association)?
- Σ Is there a prepayment penalty if I want to refinance outside at a better rate?
- Σ What happens if something happens and I default?
- Σ Will the resort help me sell if I no longer want to travel?
- Σ What are the additional fees involved?

Expect to pay additional fees involved with ownership. You will have maintenance fees to cover the costs of the staff, operations and maintenance of the resort. Out of the maintenance fees a capital fund (or reserve fund) will be put aside to cover major repairs such as a new roof, carpeting, appliances, HVAC units, furniture, swimming pool maintenance, parking lot repairs or repaving, total redecorating of the villas, etc. On the average, resorts usually strip and replace everything in a villa every five years or so.

If the owners want to add additional amenities or recreation facilities such as another pool or workout center, they bring the upgrade to the Board of Directors of the Property Owners Association and a vote is taken. If it is approved, owners may receive a special assessment, a one-time charge to cover the upgrade. And there is also the property taxes paid on your behalf to the state and local collectors. Don't be upset with these additional fees. They are put in place to keep your property as new and inviting years after you became an owner. And that is part of what this book is all about. I will show you how to write all of these expenses off. The next chapter will answer all your questions including the biggest one. **HOW???**

The bottom line here is to ask questions and only buy what you need. Believe me when I tell you. The resort will always be willing to take your money if and when you choose to upgrade in the future.

Now that we have answered a lot of the "education" questions, let's never forget the reason for the purchase in the first place. The kids!

And speaking of the kids, imagine how you can help with their education for their future. You have the ability to accomplish more in a week or two than an entire school year. And as a side note, you accomplish much for yourself also. The sharing of these times will be something you will carry with you forever.

With timeshare, you have the ability to educate yourself, your family and friends about any country you wish. What better way to learn about a different culture than to actually join them in their own backyard? You can go into over 100 countries and "live" there, still having the comforts of home. See how others live, work and play, returning home with a different outlook on the world and a better understanding of your own life. This isn't something that can be taught in schools. This can only be learned hands-on. You can offer this to yourself and others if you wish.

See over 5600 places worldwide through your own eyes instead of the eyes of others. Books can be slanted to a particular view and so can television. You can determine for yourself through your own experiences what is really going on in the world and enjoy places only dreamed of by others.

Timeshare offers the opportunity for unique educational experience by exposing owners to historical sights all over the world. You can visit St. Augustine, Florida, the oldest city in the United States, or Jamestown, Virginia, the first settlement in the United States. How about Williamsburg, Virginia to see how the original pioneers lived and worked? Or where the Boston Tea Party took place. Visit Philadelphia and see the sights of our first capital city. And for that matter, why not visit Washington, DC and experience the history of our nation? Learn about the foundation of our country, the sacrifice of those before us and the price they paid to get us here. History is to be studied and revered; we need to learn about mistakes made in the past so we will not be destined to repeat them. Visit the history of our nation and other nations while enjoying their accomplishments and treasures.

Timeshare allows your family to visit places your children are studying in History and Geography. Others can read about them while you and your children are living them. Because of you, family and friends can enjoy a more balanced, well-rounded background. As I am sure you know, book learning is limited; timeshare offers life experience. You also offer this to your current and perhaps future employer. Whom would you hire or promote? The person with just a degree and no life experience, someone with only life experience and no degree or the person with both a degree and a life experience your boss would envy? This is what timeshare can do for you.

To summarize all of this for you: **ANY TIMESHARE OWNERSHIP IS BEST FOR YOU!** Any time you can provide better vacations and stay out of concrete boxes you win. You only need to decide if you prefer a fixed week ownership, a floating week ownership, an internal points program with a week conversion or a pure points program. Any one is right when it is right for you. Research and own. You will never look back.

Experiences of life determine who we are, what we do, choices we make and memories we create. These life experiences help our health and finances along the way and provide us with friends worldwide. If life is about networking, the old phrase "not what you know but who you know," works well here. Timeshare owners, more than others, meet people from every walk of life. I wish you every success and blessing on your way to learning by experiencing all life has to offer.

CHAPTER NINE

"R" IS FOR REFERRAL TRAVEL AGENT

> And when the dollar decline makes foreign travel much more expensive, I will do more of my vacation traveling in the United States.
> ~ Martin Feldstein

Congratulations and welcome! As a timeshare owner you have become one of the elite travelers of our time. You have learned that the value of the dollar no longer matters to you. When you own a timeshare there is no longer the need to worry about inflation or the value of the dollar. You will travel anywhere at anytime because you stay at timeshare resorts. Now let me show you the miracle of timeshare ownership. You have chosen to vacation in the finest resorts worldwide with the safety and comforts of home-away-from-home. You now have the opportunity to own your timeshare and have unbelievable tax deductions. Let me show you how to take your ownership to the next level. Not only will I share with you the benefits of ownership, but I will also explain how to **write off your timeshare on your taxes**. Imagine the opportunity to write off every vacation and every expense of every trip. Let's go exploring!

Just about everyone knows you can use your vacation ownership for business lodging. But let's go to the next level. Imagine being able to write off all your vacations, airfares, car rentals, cruises, restaurants, and entertainment such as golf, diving lessons, massages, spa visits, theme park tickets, special sporting event tickets, your cable or satellite bill, the new big screen TV with DVD and stereo surround sound and anything else you can think of that has to do with travel.

Imagine the opportunity to deduct $10000-$15000-$20000-$25000-$30000 or more in new tax deductions! How would that savings help you? How much did you pay or will you pay for your timeshare ownership? If you just use your timeshare as a business expense, you can write off a percentage of your expenses. But what about your family? You are not permitted to write off their expenses.

But if you sign on with a travel agency as a **Home-Based Referral Travel Agent,** you can write off your expenses for timeshare and maintenance fees. How would you like to write off every vacation you ever go on for the rest of your life? And not only yours but your family's expenses as well. Oh, where should I begin?

You see, when travel agents travel they never travel for pleasure. They always travel for business. They go on "Fam" trips or "Familiarization" trips. How can a travel agent tell you about diving on the Great Barrier Reef in Australia unless they did it? Or what the Chocolate Spa experience is like in Hershey, Pennsylvania unless they did it? Or what the theme parks of Orlando are like unless they have been there? Or the excitement of a sports event unless they've experienced it?

Now . . . let your mind begin to wander. See the places you want to visit in your minds' eye, hear the sounds, smell the smells, touch the surroundings, experience the culture, talk to the people and taste the foods of your experience. That's it . . . use your minds' eye and put yourself right there. How do you tell someone what restaurant to try and what menu item to recommend unless you have been there and tried it? The next time you go to a restaurant, any restaurant, even those around home, notice the receipt when you pay the bill. The name of the restaurant is printed on it and the date of your visit. Now flip the receipt over to the blank side and critique the restaurant right on the back of the receipt (great atmosphere, great service, great filet mignon). You can even go back to the same restaurant as long as you try something different from the menu. Your favorite place may have a great steak but their pasta may be sub-standard. But you cannot recommend it unless you try it, correct? Think about it. If I come to your hometown and ask for a great restaurant where would you send me? And why would you send me there? And how would you know unless you tried it? What was your favorite restaurant when you went to your favorite theme park and why? And because all of your family members are employees of your home-based travel agency (yes, even your children can work for the agency as long as they are over seven years of age), you can write off their meals as a business expense with a restaurant critique, maybe a critique for kids by kids. Your children can publish their own restaurant guide for kids, by kids if they desire.

Not enough? Looking for more? How about a part of your mortgage or rent? Your business is home-based so your home office is tax deductible. Your new computer, your online connection, your cell phone, your car payments or lease, new furniture and the big screen TV with DVD/DVR and stereo surround sound are all write offs. If someone contacts your agency wanting to go to Hawaii, for example, you invite them to your home-based travel agency office, pop in a DVD about Hawaii on your new player and show your clients all they need to know to enjoy their vacation. Better yet, why not show them your digital videos of what you saw and did while you were there on your Hawaiian "Fam" Trip.

As a side note: if they want to stay in a resort instead of a hotel, do you know anyone who owns a timeshare that can be exchanged in Hawaii and rented to your clients? Hummmm.

Do you have cable or satellite TV with a travel channel? If so, part of your bill is a write off because that travel channel is now your education channel. This is where you learn about Italy, Rio, Asia, Australia, Branson, or your favorite theme park or anywhere your travel channel takes you. You can make recommendations based on the information you have mastered from this additional education.

If you play golf at any course you can now write off your games, your new clubs, and any lessons because you need the ability to tell an avid golfer what the course is really like. Want more? Ok, how's this?

Instead of paying your kids over seven years of age an allowance, pay them to work for the agency. Have them pass out business cards and flyers, do filing, critique restaurants, whatever and write off their allowance as an income. They will not have to file personal income taxes as long as they fall below the guidelines set in the Tax Code. And how about this? You have kids (or should I say young adults) in college. Every college semester has electives for additional college credits. Employers are looking for future employees that are well rounded in experience. If they take an elective that has to do with travel, they are taking the course for the family-owned business. The college course is a write off as an education expense.

How about medical insurance covering all employees of the agency? By owning the business, you are permitted to offer these benefits to your employees. You hire your family members and write off their coverage as a business expense.

How about the cruise you always dreamed of taking? Maybe you exchanged your timeshare for a cruise of your choice or you decided to pay cash at the deep discount pricing available because of your timeshare ownership. This cruise, along with the additional excursions, tours and events, is a write off because you are participating for the purpose of educating your clients.

Finally, I have found the last bastion for the "little guy:" tax benefits from their ownership. As I said, you are now one of the elite. Those that write the rules must follow the same rules as we do when it comes to the Tax Code. They are not going to make laws that hurt themselves, so **we** benefit from **their** rules.

I truly believe that the home-based travel business is the greatest tax benefit left in our time. And using your timeshare with your agency completes the total picture of being a referral travel agent. You can travel worldwide and the Tax Code will offset the costs of your deed. Use your timeshare as a tax shelter. You may receive more tax deductions than any other business or profession and have fun doing it.

I only caution you on one very important issue. ***Always, always seek professional advice on how to take advantage of your benefits! Always seek proper counsel! Pay well for this advice; it becomes priceless and your advisor is worth more than you will ever pay!*** And oh, by the way, this advice is also a write off. Life is great isn't it?

Thank you again for visiting with me through this book. If you followed me from the beginning and made it this far, you've probably learned more about me than most. If I can ever help in any way with advice, ownership, recommendations, anything, never hesitate to call or write. I am busy, but I will always answer. Just give me a little time. After all, I may be on vacation in my timeshare and writing it off so I can recommend a vacation to you (he says with a smile).

I wish you the best in life, love and experiences. Life is an adventure. Don't just TRAVEL . . . ARRIVE TODAY! Explore until the day you're called to a better "vacation."

Time to say Goodbye.

Con Té Partiro
Por Ti Volare'
(I'll Go With You).

Always and with best regards,
Keith G. Saire, CHA

P.S. If you are considering what company to join to be a referral agent might I recommend: www.ytb.com/pointstravel.

For further information please visit these sites. Anyone in the industry is more than willing to help. And yes unless it is their business, without a fee. Begin your search here!

Exchange Companies:	Redweek.com www.redweek.com
Resort Condominiums International www.rci.com	Interval International (II) www.intervalinternational.com
Hawaii www.htse.net	Platinum Interchange www. platinuminterchange.com
Donita's Dial an Exchange www.daelive.com	Trading Places International www. tradingplaces.com
Timeshare Rentals	Redweek.com www.redweek.com
Timeshare Rentals www.timesharerentals.com	Vacation Timeshare Rentals www.vacationtimesharerentals.com
My Resort Network www.myresortnetwork.com	Resortime.com www.resortime.com
Ebay Auctions www.ebay.com	Resort Rentals International www.RentingResorts.com

Timeshare Insurance
VacationGuard, Inc   www.vacationguard.com

Timeshare Financing
Tammac Financial Corporation   www.tammacfinancial.com
First Again   www.firstagain.com
Bi-Weekly Timeshare Financing (use to set up Bi-Weekly Payments)
www.biweeklytimesharefinancing.com

Referral Travel Agency Website

(In fairness of full disclosure, this site belongs to my daughter, Carrie)
Points Travel, Inc.   www.ytb.com/pointstravel

Timeshare Title and Closing Services	Timeshare Closing Services, Inc www.timeshareclosingservices.com
Transfer My Timeshare www.transfermytimeshare.com	Resort Closings, Inc www.resortclosings.com
Tri West Real Estate www.triwest-timeshare.com	Redweek.com www.redweek.com
Title Resource Group www.trgc.com	Chicago Title www.chicagotitle.com

You may contact Mr. Saire at:

Keith G. Saire, CHA
P.O. Box 692341
Orlando, Florida 32869-2341

Pointstravel@aol.com

www.ytb.com/pointstravel

Enclosed, for your convenience, are some of the forms for your CPA/Accountant/Tax Advisor. They may be outdated depending on when you purchased this book, but your advisor will know which forms to use. NOTE: I am sure there are many more deductions your advisor will recommend such as the Home Mortgage Interest. Again, please seek their advice. My CPA has saved me much more than I have ever paid him. Find a good one who is familiar with your new business and use their knowledge. The more they know, the more you benefit.

Again, permit me to add this disclaimer to make it clear to everyone:

> **Legal Disclaimer:**
>
> The author, publisher, licensee, copyright holder, and developer, in whole or in part, are not rendering tax, legal, accounting or any other factual or assumed advice. Users of this information **must seek their personal advisors** to ensure proper implementation of any ideas presented herein.

Department of the Treasury

Internal Revenue Service

Publication 527
Cat. No. 15052W

Residential Rental Property

(Including Rental of Vacation Homes)

For use in preparing
2007 Returns

Get forms and other information faster and easier by:

Internet • www.irs.gov

Contents

Reminder

Photographs of missing children. The Internal Revenue Service is a proud partner with the National Center for Missing and Exploited Children. Photographs of missing children selected by the Center may appear in this publication on pages that would otherwise be blank. You can help bring these children home by looking at the photographs and calling 1-800-THE-LOST (1-800-843-5678) if you recognize a child.

Introduction

This publication discusses rental income and expenses, including depreciation, and explains how to report them on your return. It also covers casualty losses on rental property and the passive activity and at-risk rules.

Sale of rental property. For information on how to figure and report any gain or loss from the sale or other disposition of your rental property, get Publication 544, Sales and Other Dispositions of Assets.

Sale of main home used as rental property. For information on how to figure and report any gain or loss from the sale or other disposition of your main home that you also used as rental property, get Publication 523, Selling Your Home.

Comments and suggestions. We welcome your comments about this publication and your suggestions for future editions.

You can write to us at the following address:

Internal Revenue Service
Individual Forms and Publications Branch
SE:W:CAR:MP:T:I
1111 Constitution Ave. NW, IR-6526
Washington, DC 20224

We respond to many letters by telephone. Therefore, it would be helpful if you would include your daytime phone number, including the area code, in your correspondence.

You can email us at *taxforms@irs.gov.* (The asterisk must be included in the address.) Please put "Publications Comment" on the subject line. Although we cannot respond individually to each email, we do appreciate your feedback and will consider your comments as we revise our tax products.

Ordering forms and publications. Visit *www.irs.gov/formspubs* to download forms and publications, call 1-800-829-3676, or write to the address below and receive a response within 10 days after your request is received.

National Distribution Center
P.O. Box 8903
Bloomington, IL 61702-8903

Tax questions. If you have a tax question, check the information available on *www.irs.gov* or call 1-800-829-1040. We cannot answer tax questions sent to either of the above addresses.

Useful Items

You may want to see:

Publication

- ❏ 463   Travel, Entertainment, Gift, and Car Expenses
- ❏ 534   Depreciating Property Placed in Service Before 1987
- ❏ 535   Business Expenses
- ❏ 547   Casualties, Disasters, and Thefts
- ❏ 551   Basis of Assets
- ❏ 925   Passive Activity and At-Risk Rules
- ❏ 946   How To Depreciate Property

Form (and Instructions)

- ❏ 4562   Depreciation and Amortization
- ❏ 5213   Election To Postpone Determination as To Whether the Presumption Applies That an Activity Is Engaged in for Profit
- ❏ 8582   Passive Activity Loss Limitations
- ❏ Schedule E (Form 1040) Supplemental Income and Loss

See *How To Get Tax Help* at the end of this publication for information about getting these publications and forms.

Rental Income

You generally must include in your gross income all amounts you receive as rent. Rental income is any payment you receive for the use or occupation of property. In addition to amounts you receive as normal rent payments, there are other amounts, discussed later, that may be rental income.

When to report. When you report rental income on your return depends on whether you are a cash basis taxpayer or use an accrual method.

If you are a cash basis taxpayer, you report rental income on your return for the year you actually or constructively receive it. You are a cash basis taxpayer if you report income in the year you receive it, regardless of when it was earned. You constructively receive income when it is made available to you, for example, by being credited to your bank account.

If you use an accrual method, you generally report income when you earn it, rather than when you receive it. You generally deduct your expenses when you incur them, rather than when you pay them.

For more information about when you constructively receive income and accrual methods of accounting, see Publication 538, Accounting Periods and Methods.

Advance rent. Advance rent is any amount you receive before the period that it covers. Include advance rent in your rental income in the year you receive it regardless of the period covered or the method of accounting you use.

Example. You sign a 10-year lease to rent your property. In the first year, you receive $5,000 for the first year's rent and $5,000 as rent for the last year of the lease. You must include $10,000 in your income in the first year.

Security deposits. Do not include a security deposit in your income when you receive it if you plan to return it to your tenant at the end of the lease. But if you keep part or all of the security deposit during any year because your tenant does not live up to the terms of the lease, include the amount you keep in your income in that year.

If an amount called a security deposit is to be used as a final payment of rent, it is advance rent. Include it in your income when you receive it.

Payment for canceling a lease. If your tenant pays you to cancel a lease, the amount you receive is rent. Include the payment in your income in the year you receive it regardless of your method of accounting.

Expenses paid by tenant. If your tenant pays any of your expenses, the payments are rental income. You must include them in your income. You can deduct the expenses if they are deductible rental expenses. See *Rental Expenses,* later, for more information.

Example 1. Your tenant pays the water and sewage bill for your rental property and deducts it from the normal rent payment. Under the terms of the lease, your tenant does not have to pay this bill. Include the utility bill paid by the tenant and any amount received as a rent payment in your rental income. You can deduct the utility payment made by your tenant as a rental expense.

Example 2. While you are out of town, the furnace in your rental property stops working. Your tenant pays for the necessary repairs and deducts the repair bill from the rent payment. Include the repair bill paid by the tenant and any amount received as a rent payment in your rental income. You can deduct the repair payment made by your tenant as a rental expense.

Property or services. If you receive property or services, instead of money, as rent, include the fair market value of the property or services in your rental income.

If the services are provided at an agreed upon or specified price, that price is the fair market value unless there is evidence to the contrary.

Example. Your tenant is a painter. He offers to paint your rental property instead of paying 2 months' rent. You accept his offer.

Include in your rental income the amount the tenant would have paid for 2 months' rent. You can deduct that same amount as a rental expense for painting your property.

Lease with option to buy. If the rental agreement gives your tenant the right to buy your rental property, the payments you receive under the agreement are generally rental income. If your tenant exercises the right to buy the property, the payments you receive for the period after the date of sale are considered part of the selling price.

Rental of property also used as a home. If you rent property that you also use as your home and you rent it fewer than 15 days during the tax year, do not include the rent you receive in your income and do not deduct rental expenses. However, you can deduct on Schedule A (Form 1040) the interest, taxes, and casualty and theft losses that are allowed for nonrental property. See *Personal Use of Dwelling Unit (Including Vacation Home),* later.

Part interest. If you own a part interest in rental property, you must report your part of the rental income from the property.

Rental Expenses

This section discusses expenses of renting property that you ordinarily can deduct from your rental income. It includes information on the expenses you can deduct if you rent a condominium or cooperative apartment, if you rent part of your property, or if you change your property to rental use. Depreciation, which you can also deduct from your rental income, is discussed later under *Depreciation.*

When to deduct. You generally deduct your rental expenses in the year you pay them.

Vacant rental property. If you hold property for rental purposes, you may be able to deduct your ordinary and necessary expenses (including depreciation) for managing, conserving, or maintaining the property while the property is vacant. However, you cannot deduct any loss of rental income for the period the property is vacant.

Pre-rental expenses. You can deduct your ordinary and necessary expenses for managing, conserving, or maintaining rental property from the time you make it available for rent.

Depreciation. You can begin to depreciate rental property when it is ready and available for rent. See *Placed-in-Service Date* under *Depreciation*, later.

Expenses for rental property sold. If you sell property you held for rental purposes, you can deduct the ordinary and necessary expenses for managing, conserving, or maintaining the property until it is sold.

Personal use of rental property. If you sometimes use your rental property for personal purposes, you must divide your expenses between rental and personal use. Also, your rental expense deductions may be limited. See *Personal Use of Dwelling Unit (Including Vacation Home)*, later.

Part interest. If you own a part interest in rental property, you can deduct your part of the expenses that you paid.

Uncollected rent. If you are a cash basis taxpayer, you do not report uncollected rent. Because you do not include it in your income, you cannot deduct it.

If you use an accrual method, you report income when you earn it. If you are unable to collect the rent, you may be able to deduct it as a business bad debt. See chapter 10 of Publication 535 for more information about business bad debts.

Repairs and Improvements

You can deduct the cost of repairs to your rental property. You cannot deduct the cost of improvements. You recover the cost of improvements by taking depreciation (explained later).

Separate the costs of repairs and improvements, and keep accurate records. You will need to know the cost of improvements when you sell or depreciate your property.

Repairs. A repair keeps your property in good operating condition. It does not materially add to the value of your property or substantially prolong its life. Repainting your property inside or out, fixing gutters or floors, fixing leaks, plastering, and replacing broken windows are examples of repairs.

If you make repairs as part of an extensive remodeling or restoration of your property, the whole job is an improvement.

Improvements. An improvement adds to the value of property, prolongs its useful life, or adapts it to new uses. Table 1 shows examples of many improvements.

If you make an improvement to property, the cost of the improvement must be capitalized. The capitalized cost can generally be depreciated as if the improvement were separate property.

Other Expenses

In addition to depreciation and the cost of repairs, you can deduct the following expenses from your rental income.

- Advertising.
- Cleaning and maintenance.
- Utilities.
- Insurance.

- Taxes.
- Interest.
- Points.
- Commissions.
- Tax return preparation fees.
- Travel expenses.
- Rental payments.
- Local transportation expenses.

Some of these expenses are discussed next.

Rental payments for property. You can deduct the rent you pay for property that you use for rental purposes. If you buy a leasehold for rental purposes, you can deduct an equal part of the cost each year over the term of the lease.

Rental of equipment. You can deduct the rent you pay for equipment that you use for rental purposes. However, in some cases, lease contracts are actually purchase contracts. If so, you cannot deduct these payments. You can recover the cost of purchased equipment through depreciation.

Insurance premiums paid in advance. If you pay an insurance premium for more than one year in advance, each year you can deduct the part of the premium payment that will apply to that year. You cannot deduct the total premium in the year you pay it.

Local benefit taxes. Generally, you cannot deduct charges for local benefits that increase the value of your property, such as charges for putting in streets, sidewalks, or water and sewer systems. These charges are nondepreciable capital expenditures. You must add them to the basis of your property. You can deduct local benefit taxes if they are for maintaining, repairing, or paying interest charges for the benefits.

Interest expense. You can deduct mortgage interest you pay on your rental property. Chapter 4 of Publication 535 explains mortgage interest in detail.

Expenses paid to obtain a mortgage. Certain expenses you pay to obtain a mortgage on your rental property cannot be deducted as interest. These expenses, which include mortgage commissions, abstract fees, and recording fees, are capital expenses. However, you can amortize them over the life of the mortgage.

Form 1098. If you paid $600 or more of mortgage interest on your rental property to any one person, you should receive a Form 1098, Mortgage Interest Statement, or similar statement showing the interest you paid for the year. If you and at least one other person (other than your spouse if you file a joint return) were liable for, and paid interest on, the mortgage, and the other person received the Form 1098, report your share of the interest on Schedule E (Form 1040), line 13. Attach a statement to your return showing the name and address of the other person. In the left margin of Schedule E, next to line 13, enter "See attached."

Points. The term "points" is often used to describe some of the charges paid by a borrower to take out a loan or a mortgage. These charges are also called loan origination fees, maximum loan charges, or premium charges. If

Table 1. Examples of Improvements

Caution. Work you do (or have done) on your home that does not add much to either the value or the life of the property, but rather keeps the property in good condition, is considered a repair, not an improvement.

Additions	Heating & Air Conditioning
Bedroom	Heating system
Bathroom	Central air conditioning
Deck	Furnace
Garage	Duct work
Porch	Central humidifier
Patio	Filtration system
Lawn & Grounds	**Plumbing**
Landscaping	Septic system
Driveway	Water heater
Walkway	Soft water system
Fence	Filtration system
Retaining wall	
Sprinkler system	**Interior Improvements**
Swimming pool	Built-in appliances
	Kitchen modernization
Miscellaneous	Flooring
Storm windows, doors	Wall-to-wall carpeting
New roof	
Central vacuum	**Insulation**
Wiring upgrades	Attic
Satellite dish	Walls, floor
Security system	Pipes, duct work

any of these charges (points) are solely for the use of money, they are interest.

Points paid when you take out a loan or mortgage result in original issue discount (OID). In general, the points (OID) are deductible as interest unless they must be capitalized. How you figure the amount of points (OID) you can deduct each year depends on whether or not your total OID, including the OID resulting from the points, is insignificant or de minimis. If the OID is not de minimis, you must use the constant-yield method to figure how much you can deduct.

De minimis OID. The OID is de minimis if it is less than one-fourth of 1% (.0025) of the stated redemption price at maturity multiplied by the number of full years from the date of original issue to maturity (the term of the loan).

If the OID is de minimis, you can choose one of the following ways to figure the amount you can deduct each year.

* On a constant-yield basis over the term of the loan.

* On a straight line basis over the term of the loan.

* In proportion to stated interest payments.

* In its entirety at maturity of the loan.

You make this choice by deducting the OID in a manner consistent with the method chosen on your timely filed tax return for the tax year in which the loan is issued.

Example of de minimis amount. On January 1, 2007, you took out a loan for $100,000. The loan matures on January 1, 2017 (a 10-year term), and the stated principal amount of the loan ($100,000) is payable on that date. An interest payment of $10,000 is payable to the bank on January 2 of each year, beginning on January 2, 2008. When the loan was made, you paid $1,500 in points to the bank. The points reduced the issue price of the loan from $100,000 to $98,500, resulting in $1,500 of OID. You determine that the points (OID) you paid are de minimis based on the following computation.

Redemption price at maturity
(principal amount of the loan)	$100,000
Multiplied by: The term of the loan in complete years	× 10
Multiplied by	× .0025
De minimis amount	$ 2,500

The points (OID) you paid ($1,500) are less than the de minimis amount. Therefore, you have de minimis OID and you can choose one of the four ways discussed earlier to figure the amount you can deduct each year. Under the straight line method, you can deduct $150 each year for 10 years.

Constant-yield method. If the OID is not de minimis, you must use the constant-yield method to figure how much you can deduct each year.

You figure your deduction for the first year in the following manner.

1. Determine the issue price of the loan. Generally, this equals the proceeds of the loan. If you paid points on the loan, the issue price generally is the difference between the proceeds and the points.

2. Multiply the result in (1) by the yield to maturity.

3. Subtract any qualified stated interest payments from the result in (2). This is the OID you can deduct in the first year.

To figure your deduction in any subsequent year, you start with the adjusted issue price. To get the adjusted issue price, add to the issue price any OID previously deducted. Then follow steps (2) and (3) above.

The yield to maturity (YTM) is generally shown in the literature you receive from your lender. If you do not have this information, consult your lender or tax advisor. In general, the YTM is the discount rate that, when used in computing the present value of all principal and interest payments, produces an amount equal to the principal amount of the loan.

Qualified stated interest (QSI) is stated interest that is unconditionally payable in cash or property (other than another loan of the issuer) at least annually over the term of the loan at a single fixed rate.

Example of constant yield. The facts are the same as in the previous example. The yield to maturity on your loan is 10.2467%, compounded annually.

You figure the amount of points (OID) you can deduct in 2007 as follows.

Principal amount of the loan	$100,000
Minus: Points	1,500
Issue price of the loan	$ 98,500
Multiplied by: YTM	× .102467
Total	10,093
Minus: QSI	10,000
Points (OID) deductible in 2007	$ 93

You figure the deduction for 2008 as follows.

Issue price	$98,500
Plus: Points (OID) deducted in 2007	93
Adjusted issue price	$98,593
Multiplied by: YTM	× .102467
Total	10,103
Minus: QSI	10,000
Points (OID) deductible in 2008 . .	$ 103

Loan or mortgage ends. If your loan or mortgage ends, you may be able to deduct any remaining points (OID) in the tax year in which the loan or mortgage ends. A loan or mortgage may end due to a refinancing, prepayment, foreclosure, or similar event. However, if the refinancing is with the same lender, the remaining points (OID) generally are not deductible in the year in which the refinancing occurs, but may be deductible over the term of the new mortgage or loan.

Travel expenses. You can deduct the ordinary and necessary expenses of traveling away from home if the primary purpose of the trip was to collect rental income or to manage, conserve, or maintain your rental property. You must properly allocate your expenses between rental and nonrental activities. You cannot deduct the cost of traveling away from home if the primary purpose of the trip was the improvement of your property. You recover the cost of improvements by taking depreciation. For information on travel expenses, see chapter 1 of Publication 463.

 To deduct travel expenses, you must keep records that follow the rules in chapter 5 of Publication 463.

Local transportation expenses. You can deduct your ordinary and necessary local transportation expenses if you incur them to collect rental income or to manage, conserve, or maintain your rental property.

Generally, if you use your personal car, pickup truck, or light van for rental activities, you can deduct the expenses using one of two methods: actual expenses or the standard mileage rate. For 2007, the standard mileage rate is 48½ cents a mile for all business miles. For more information, see chapter 4 of Publication 463.

To deduct car expenses under either method, you must keep records that follow the rules in chapter 5 of Publication 463. In addition, you must complete Form 4562, Part V, and attach it to your tax return.

Tax return preparation. You can deduct, as a rental expense, the part of tax return preparation fees you paid to prepare Schedule E (Form 1040), Part I. For example, on your 2007 Schedule E you can deduct fees paid in 2007 to prepare Part I of your 2006 Schedule E. You can also deduct, as a rental expense, any expense (other than federal taxes and penalties) you paid to resolve a tax underpayment related to your rental activities.

Condominiums and Cooperatives

If you rent out a condominium or a cooperative apartment, special rules apply. Condominiums are treated differently from cooperatives.

Condominium

If you own a condominium, you own a dwelling unit in a multi-unit building. You also own a share of the common elements of the structure, such as land, lobbies, elevators, and service areas. You and the other condominium owners may pay dues or assessments to a special corporation that is organized to take care of the common elements.

If you rent your condominium to others, you can deduct:

* Depreciation,

* Repairs,

* Upkeep,

* Dues,

* Interest and taxes, and

* Assessments for the care of the common parts of the structure.

You cannot deduct special assessments you pay to a condominium management corporation for improvements. But you may be able to recover your share of the cost of any improvement by taking depreciation.

Cooperative

If you have a cooperative apartment that you rent to others, you can usually deduct, as a rental expense, all the maintenance fees you pay to the cooperative housing corporation. However, you cannot deduct a payment earmarked for a capital asset or improvement, or otherwise charged to the corporation's capital account. For example, you cannot deduct a payment used to pave a community parking lot, install a new roof, or pay the principal of the corporation's mortgage. You must add the payment to the basis of your stock in the corporation.

Treat as a capital cost the amount you were assessed for capital items. This cannot be more than the amount by which your payments to the corporation exceeded your share of the corporation's mortgage interest and real estate taxes.

Your share of interest and taxes is the amount the corporation elected to allocate to you, if it reasonably reflects those expenses for your apartment. Otherwise, figure your share in the following way.

1. Divide the number of your shares of stock by the total number of shares outstanding, including any shares held by the corporation.

2. Multiply the corporation's deductible interest by the number you figured in (1). This is your share of the interest.

3. Multiply the corporation's deductible taxes by the number you figured in (1). This is your share of the taxes.

In addition to the maintenance fees paid to the cooperative housing corporation, you can deduct your direct payments for repairs, upkeep, and other rental expenses, including interest paid on a loan used to buy your stock in the corporation. The depreciation deduction allowed for cooperative apartments is discussed at *Cooperative apartments*, under *Depreciation*, later.

Not Rented for Profit

If you do not rent your property to make a profit, you can deduct your rental expenses only up to the amount of your rental income. You cannot carry forward to the next year any rental expenses that are more than your rental income for the year. For more information about the rules for an activity not engaged in for profit, see *Not-for-Profit Activities* in chapter 1 of Publication 535.

Where to report. Report your not-for-profit rental income on Form 1040 or Form 1040NR, line 21. You can include your mortgage interest and any qualified mortgage insurance premiums (if you use the property as your main home or second home), real estate taxes, and casualty losses on the appropriate lines of Schedule A (Form 1040) if you itemize your deductions.

Claim your other rental expenses, subject to the rules explained in chapter 1 of Publication 535, as miscellaneous itemized deductions on line 23 of Schedule A (Form 1040). You can deduct these expenses only if they, together with certain other miscellaneous itemized deductions, total more than 2% of your adjusted gross income.

Postponing decision. If your rental income is more than your rental expenses for at least 3 years out of a period of 5 consecutive years, you

are presumed to be renting your property to make a profit. You may choose to postpone the decision of whether the rental is for profit by filing Form 5213.

See Publication 535 for more information.

Property Changed to Rental Use

If you change your home or other property (or a part of it) to rental use at any time other than the beginning of your tax year, you must divide yearly expenses, such as taxes and insurance, between rental use and personal use.

You can deduct as rental expenses only the part of the expense that is for the part of the year the property was used or held for rental purposes.

For depreciation purposes, treat the property as being placed in service on the conversion date.

You cannot deduct depreciation or insurance for the part of the year the property was held for personal use. However, you can include the home mortgage interest, qualified mortgage insurance premiums, and real estate tax expenses for the part of the year the property was held for personal use as an itemized deduction on Schedule A (Form 1040).

Example. Your tax year is the calendar year. You moved from your home in May and started renting it out on June 1. You can deduct as rental expenses seven-twelfths of your yearly expenses, such as taxes and insurance.

Starting with June, you can deduct as rental expenses the amounts you pay for items generally billed monthly, such as utilities.

When figuring depreciation, treat the property as placed in service on June 1.

Renting Part of Property

If you rent part of your property, you must divide certain expenses between the part of the property used for rental purposes and the part of the property used for personal purposes, as though you actually had two separate pieces of property.

You can deduct the expenses related to the part of the property used for rental purposes, such as home mortgage interest, qualified mortgage insurance premiums, and real estate taxes, as rental expenses on Schedule E (Form 1040). You can also deduct as a rental expense a part of other expenses that normally are nondeductible personal expenses, such as expenses for electricity, or painting the outside of your house.

You can deduct the expenses for the part of the property used for personal purposes, subject to certain limitations, only if you itemize your deductions on Schedule A (Form 1040).

You cannot deduct any part of the cost of the first phone line even if your tenants have unlimited use of it.

You do not have to divide the expenses that belong only to the rental part of your property.

For example, if you paint a room that you rent, or if you pay premiums for liability insurance in connection with renting a room in your home, your entire cost is a rental expense. If you install a second phone line strictly for your tenant's use, all of the cost of the second line is deductible as a rental expense. You can deduct depreciation, discussed later, on the part of the property used for rental purposes as well as on the furniture and equipment you use for rental purposes.

How to divide expenses. If an expense is for both rental use and personal use, such as mortgage interest or heat for the entire house, you must divide the expense between rental use and personal use. You can use any reasonable method for dividing the expense. It may be reasonable to divide the cost of some items (for example, water) based on the number of people using them. However, the two most common methods for dividing an expense are one based on the number of rooms in your home and one based on the square footage of your home.

Example. You rent a room in your house. The room is 12 × 15 feet, or 180 square feet. Your entire house has 1,800 square feet of floor space. You can deduct as a rental expense 10% of any expense that must be divided between rental use and personal use. If your heating bill for the year for the entire house was $600, $60 ($600 × 10%) is a rental expense. The balance, $540, is a personal expense that you cannot deduct.

Personal Use of Dwelling Unit (Including Vacation Home)

If you have any personal use of a dwelling unit (defined later) (including a vacation home) that you rent, you must divide your expenses between rental use and personal use. See *Figuring Days of Personal Use* and *How To Divide Expenses*, later.

If you used a dwelling unit for personal purposes, it may be considered a "dwelling unit used as a home." If it is, you cannot deduct rental expenses that are more than your rental income for the unit. See *Dwelling Unit Used as Home* and *How To Figure Rental Income and Deductions*, later. If the dwelling unit is not considered a dwelling unit used as a home, you can deduct rental expenses that are more than your rental income for the unit, subject to certain limits. See *Limits on Rental Losses*, later.

Exception for minimal rental use. If you use the dwelling unit as a home and you rent it fewer than 15 days during the year, do not include any of the rent in your income and do not deduct any of the rental expenses. See *Dwelling Unit Used as Home*, later.

Dwelling unit. A dwelling unit includes a house, apartment, condominium, mobile home, boat, vacation home, or similar property. A dwelling unit has basic living accommodations, such as sleeping space, a toilet, and cooking facilities. A dwelling unit does not include property used solely as a hotel, motel, inn, or similar establishment.

Property is used solely as a hotel, motel, inn, or similar establishment if it is regularly available for occupancy by paying customers and is not used by an owner as a home during the year.

Example. You rent a room in your home that is always available for short-term occupancy by paying customers. You do not use the room yourself and you allow only paying customers to use the room. The room is used solely as a hotel, motel, inn, or similar establishment and is not a dwelling unit.

Dwelling Unit Used as Home

The tax treatment of rental income and expenses for a dwelling unit that you also use for personal purposes depends on whether you use it as a home. (See *How To Figure Rental Income and Deductions*, later).

You use a dwelling unit as a home during the tax year if you use it for personal purposes more than the greater of:

1. 14 days, or

2. 10% of the total days it is rented to others at a fair rental price.

See *Figuring Days of Personal Use*, later.

If a dwelling unit is used for personal purposes on a day it is rented at a fair rental price, do not count that day as a day of rental use in applying (2) above. Instead, count it as a day of personal use in applying both (1) and (2) above. This rule does not apply when dividing expenses between rental and personal use.

Fair rental price. A fair rental price for your property generally is the amount of rent that a person who is not related to you would be willing to pay. The rent you charge is not a fair rental price if it is substantially less than the rents charged for other properties that are similar to your property.

Ask yourself the following questions when comparing another property with yours.

- Is it used for the same purpose?
- Is it approximately the same size?
- Is it in approximately the same condition?
- Does it have similar furnishings?
- Is it in a similar location?

If any of the answers are no, the properties probably are not similar.

Examples

The following examples show how to determine whether you used your rental property as a home.

Example 1. You converted the basement of your home into an apartment with a bedroom, a bathroom, and a small kitchen. You rented the basement apartment at a fair rental price to college students during the regular school year. You rented to them on a 9-month lease (273 days). You figured 10% of the total days rented to others at a fair rental price is 27 days.

During June (30 days), your brothers stayed with you and lived in the basement apartment rent free.

Your basement apartment was used as a home because you used it for personal purposes for 30 days. Rent-free use by your brothers is considered personal use. Your personal use (30 days) is more than the greater of 14 days or 10% of the total days it was rented (27 days).

Example 2. You rented the guest bedroom in your home at a fair rental price during the local college's homecoming, commencement, and football weekends (a total of 27 days). Your sister-in-law stayed in the room, rent free, for the last 3 weeks (21 days) in July. You figured 10% of the total days rented to others at a fair rental price is 3 days.

The room was used as a home because you used it for personal purposes for 21 days. That is more than the greater of 14 days or 10% of the 27 days it was rented (3 days).

Example 3. You own a condominium apartment in a resort area. You rented it at a fair rental price for a total of 170 days during the year. For 12 of these days, the tenant was not able to use the apartment and allowed you to use it even though you did not refund any of the rent. Your family actually used the apartment for 10 of those days. Therefore, the apartment is treated as having been rented for 160 (170 − 10) days. You figure 10% of the total days rented to others at a fair rental price is 16 days. Your family also used the apartment for 7 other days during the year.

You used the apartment as a home because you used it for personal purposes for 17 days. That is more than the greater of 14 days or 10% of the 160 days it was rented (16 days).

Use as Main Home Before or After Renting

For purposes of determining whether a dwelling unit was used as a home, you may not have to count days you used the property as your main home before or after renting it or offering it for rent as days of personal use. Do not count them as days of personal use if:

- You rented or tried to rent the property for 12 or more consecutive months.

- You rented or tried to rent the property for a period of less than 12 consecutive months and the period ended because you sold or exchanged the property.

This special rule does not apply when dividing expenses between rental and personal use.

Example 1. On February 28, you moved out of the house you had lived in for 6 years because you accepted a job in another town. You rent your house at a fair rental price from March 15 of that year to May 14 of the next year (14 months). On the following June 1, you move back into your old house.

The days you used the house as your main home from January 1 to February 28 and from June 1 to December 31 of the next year are not counted as days of personal use.

Example 2. On January 31, you moved out of the condominium where you had lived for 3 years. You offered it for rent at a fair rental price beginning on February 1. You were unable to rent it until April. On September 15, you sold the condominium.

The days you used the condominium as your main home from January 1 to January 31 are not counted as days of personal use when determining whether you used it as a home.

Figuring Days of Personal Use

A day of personal use of a dwelling unit is any day that the unit is used by any of the following persons.

1. You or any other person who has an interest in it, unless you rent it to another owner as his or her main home under a shared equity financing agreement (defined later). However, see *Use as Main Home Before or After Renting* under *Dwelling Unit Used As Home*, earlier.

2. A member of your family or a member of the family of any other person who has an interest in it, unless the family member uses the dwelling unit as his or her main home and pays a fair rental price. Family includes only brothers and sisters, half-brothers and half-sisters, spouses, ancestors (parents, grandparents, etc.) and lineal descendants (children, grandchildren, etc.).

3. Anyone under an arrangement that lets you use some other dwelling unit.

4. Anyone at less than a fair rental price.

Main home. If the other person or member of the family in (1) or (2) above has more than one home, his or her main home is ordinarily the one he or she lived in most of the time.

Shared equity financing agreement. This is an agreement under which two or more persons acquire undivided interests for more than 50 years in an entire dwelling unit, including the land, and one or more of the co-owners is entitled to occupy the unit as his or her main home upon payment of rent to the other co-owner or owners.

Donation of use of property. You use a dwelling unit for personal purposes if:

- You donate the use of the unit to a charitable organization,
- The organization sells the use of the unit at a fund-raising event, and
- The "purchaser" uses the unit.

Examples

The following examples show how to determine days of personal use.

Example 1. You and your neighbor are co-owners of a condominium at the beach. You rent the unit to vacationers whenever possible. The unit is not used as a main home by anyone. Your neighbor uses the unit for 2 weeks every year.

Publication 527 (2007)

Because your neighbor has an interest in the unit, both of you are considered to have used the unit for personal purposes during those 2 weeks.

Example 2. You and your neighbors are co-owners of a house under a shared equity financing agreement. Your neighbors live in the house and pay you a fair rental price.

Even though your neighbors have an interest in the house, the days your neighbors live there are not counted as days of personal use by you. This is because your neighbors rent the house as their main home under a shared equity financing agreement.

Example 3. You own a rental property that you rent to your son. Your son has no interest in this property. He uses it as his main home. He pays you a fair rental price for the property.

Your son's use of the property is not personal use by you because your son is using it as his main home, he has no interest in the property, and he is paying you a fair rental price.

Example 4. You rent your beach house to Rosa. Rosa rents her house in the mountains to you. You each pay a fair rental price.

You are using your house for personal purposes on the days that Rosa uses it because your house is used by Rosa under an arrangement that allows you to use her house.

Example 5. You rent an apartment to your mother at less than a fair rental price. You are using the apartment for personal purposes on the days that your mother rents it because you rent it for less than a fair rental price.

Days Used for
Repairs and Maintenance

Any day that you spend working substantially full time repairing and maintaining (not improving) your property is not counted as a day of personal use. Do not count such a day as a day of personal use even if family members use the property for recreational purposes on the same day.

Example. You own a cabin in the mountains that you rent during the summer. You spend 3 days at the cabin each May, working full time to repair anything that was damaged over the winter and get the cabin ready for the summer. You also spend 3 days each September, working full time to repair any damage done by renters and getting the cabin ready for the winter.

These 6 days do not count as days of personal use even if your family uses the cabin while you are repairing it.

How To Divide Expenses

If you use a dwelling unit for both rental and personal purposes, divide your expenses between the rental use and the personal use based on the number of days used for each purpose. You can deduct expenses for the rental use of the unit under the rules explained in *How To Figure Rental Income and Deductions,* later.

When dividing your expenses, follow these rules.

- Any day that the unit is rented at a fair rental price is a day of rental use even if you used the unit for personal purposes that day. This rule does not apply when determining whether you used the unit as a home.

- Any day that the unit is available for rent but not actually rented is not a day of rental use.

Example. Your beach cottage was available for rent from June 1 through August 31 (92 days). Your family uses the cottage during the last 2 weeks in May (14 days). You were unable to find a renter for the first week in August (7 days). The person who rented the cottage for July allowed you to use it over a weekend (2 days) without any reduction in or refund of rent. The cottage was not used at all before May 17 or after August 31.

You figure the part of the cottage expenses to treat as rental expenses as follows.

- The cottage was used for rental a total of 85 days (92 − 7). The days it was available for rent but not rented (7 days) are not days of rental use. The July weekend (2 days) you used it is rental use because you received a fair rental price for the weekend.

- You used the cottage for personal purposes for 14 days (the last 2 weeks in May).

- The total use of the cottage was 99 days (14 days personal use + 85 days rental use).

- Your rental expenses are 85/99 (86%) of the cottage expenses.

When determining whether you used the cottage as a home, the July weekend (2 days) you used it is personal use even though you received a fair rental price for the weekend. Therefore, you had 16 days of personal use and 83 days of rental use for this purpose. Because you used the cottage for personal purposes more than 14 days and more than 10% of the days of rental use (8 days), you may not be able to deduct all of the rental expenses. See *Property Used as a Home* in the following discussion.

How To Figure Rental
Income and Deductions

How you figure your rental income and deductions depends on whether you used the dwelling unit as a home (see *Dwelling Unit Used as Home,* earlier) and, if you used it as a home, how many days the property was rented at a fair rental price.

Property Not Used as a Home

If you do not use a dwelling unit as a home, report all the rental income and deduct all the rental expenses. See *How To Report Rental Income and Expenses,* later.

Your deductible rental expenses can be more than your gross rental income. However, see *Limits on Rental Losses,* later.

Property Used as a Home

If you use a dwelling unit as a home during the year, how you figure your rental income and deductions depends on how many days the unit was rented at a fair rental price.

Rented fewer than 15 days. If you use a dwelling unit as a home and you rent it fewer than 15 days during the year, do not include any rental income in your income. Also, you cannot deduct any expenses as rental expenses.

Rented 15 days or more. If you use a dwelling unit as a home and rent it 15 days or more during the year, you include all your rental income in your income. See *How To Report Rental Income and Expenses,* later. If you had a net profit from the rental property for the year (that is, if your rental income is more than the total of your rental expenses, including depreciation), deduct all of your rental expenses. However, if you had a net loss, your deduction for certain rental expenses is limited.

Limit on deductions. If your rental expenses are more than your rental income, you cannot use the excess expenses to offset income from other sources. The excess can be carried forward to the next year and treated as rental expenses for the same property. Any expenses carried forward to next year will be subject to any limits that apply next year. You can deduct the expenses carried over to a year only up to the amount of your rental income for that year, even if you do not use the property as your home for that year.

To figure your deductible rental expenses and any carryover to next year, use Worksheet 1.

Depreciation

You recover the cost of income producing property through yearly tax deductions. You do this by depreciating the property; that is, by deducting some of the cost on the tax return each year.

Three basic factors determine how much depreciation you can deduct. They are: (1) your basis in the property, (2) the recovery period for the property, and (3) the depreciation method used. You cannot simply deduct your mortgage or principal payments, or the cost of furniture, fixtures and equipment, as an expense.

You can deduct depreciation only on the part of your property used for rental purposes. Depreciation reduces your basis for figuring gain or loss on a later sale or exchange.

You may have to use Form 4562 to figure and report your depreciation. See *How To Report Rental Income and Expenses,* later. Also see Publication 946.

Claiming the correct amount of depreciation. You should claim the correct amount of depreciation each tax year. Even if you did not claim depreciation that you were entitled to deduct, you must still reduce your basis in the property by the full amount of depreciation that you could have deducted. See *Decreases to basis,* later, under *Adjusted Basis* for more information. If you did not deduct the correct amount of depreciation for property in any year, you may be able to make a correction for that year by filing Form 1040X, Amended U.S. Individual Income Tax

Worksheet 1. **Worksheet for Figuring Rental Deductions for a Dwelling Unit Used as a Home**

Keep for Your Records

Use this worksheet only if you answer "yes" to all the following questions.
- Did you use the dwelling unit as a home this year? (See *Dwelling Unit Used as Home*.)
- Did you rent the dwelling unit 15 days or more this year?
- Is the total of your rental expenses and depreciation more than your rental income?

1.	Enter rents received	
2a.	Enter the rental portion of deductible home mortgage interest and qualified mortgage insurance premiums (see instructions)	
b.	Enter the rental portion of real estate taxes	
c.	Enter the rental portion of deductible casualty and theft losses (see instructions)	
d.	Enter direct rental expenses (see instructions)	
e.	**Fully deductible rental expenses.** Add lines 2a–2d (see instructions)	
3.	Subtract line 2e from line 1. If zero or less, enter -0-	
4a.	Enter the rental portion of expenses directly related to operating or maintaining the dwelling unit (such as repairs, insurance, and utilities)	
b.	Enter the rental portion of excess mortgage interest and qualified mortgage insurance premiums (see instructions)	
c.	Add lines 4a and 4b	
d.	**Allowable expenses.** Enter the smaller of line 3 or line 4c (see instructions)	
5.	Subtract line 4d from line 3. If zero or less, enter -0-	
6a.	Enter the rental portion of excess casualty and theft losses (see instructions)	
b.	Enter the rental portion of depreciation of the dwelling unit	
c.	Add lines 6a and 6b	
d.	**Allowable excess casualty and theft losses and depreciation.** Enter the smaller of line 5 or line 6c (see instructions)	
7a.	Operating expenses to be carried over to next year. Subtract line 4d from line 4c	
b.	Excess casualty and theft losses and depreciation to be carried over to next year. Subtract line 6d from line 6c	

Worksheet Instructions

Follow these instructions for the worksheet above. To find the rental portion of your expenses for lines 2a–2c, 4a–4b, and 6a–6b, follow the directions given earlier under *How To Divide Expenses*. If you were unable to deduct all your expenses last year because of the rental income limit, add these unused amounts to your expenses for this year.

Line 2a. Figure the mortgage interest on the dwelling unit that you could deduct on Schedule A (Form 1040) if you had not rented the unit. Do not include interest on a loan that did not benefit the dwelling unit. For example, do not include interest on a home equity loan used to pay off credit cards or other personal loans, buy a car, or pay college tuition. Include interest on a loan used to buy, build, or improve the dwelling unit, or to refinance such a loan. Include the rental portion of this interest in the total you enter on line 2a of the worksheet.

Figure the qualified mortgage insurance premiums on the dwelling unit that you could deduct on line 13 of Schedule A (Form 1040), if you had not rented the unit. See page A-7 of the Schedule A (Form 1040) instructions. However, figure your adjusted gross income (Form 1040, line 38) without your rental income and expenses from the dwelling unit. See *Line 4b* below to deduct part of the qualified mortgage insurance premiums not allowed because of the adjusted gross income limit. Include the rental portion of the amount from Schedule A, line 13, in the total you enter on line 2a of the worksheet.

Note. Do not file this Schedule A or use it to figure the amount to deduct on line 13 of that schedule. Instead, figure the personal portion on a separate Schedule A.

Line 2c. Figure the casualty and theft losses related to the dwelling unit that you could deduct on Schedule A (Form 1040) if you had not rented the dwelling unit. To do this, complete Form 4684, Casualties and Thefts, Section A, treating the losses as personal losses. On Form 4684, line 17, enter 10% of your adjusted gross income figured without your rental income and expenses from the dwelling unit. Enter the rental portion of the result from Form 4684, line 18, on line 2c of this worksheet.

Note. Do not file this Form 4684 or use it to figure your personal losses on Schedule A. Instead, figure the personal portion on a separate Form 4684.

Line 2d. Enter the total of your rental expenses that are directly related only to the rental activity. These include interest on loans used for rental activities other than to buy, build, or improve the dwelling unit. Also include rental agency fees, advertising, office supplies, and depreciation on office equipment used in your rental activity.

Line 2e. You can deduct the amounts on lines 2a, 2b, 2c, and 2d as rental expenses on Schedule E even if your rental expenses are more than your rental income. Enter the amounts on lines 2a, 2b, 2c, and 2d on the appropriate lines of Schedule E.

Line 4b. On line 2a, you entered the rental portion of the mortgage interest and qualified mortgage insurance premiums you could deduct on Schedule A if you had not rented the dwelling unit. Enter on line 4b of this worksheet the rental portion of the mortgage interest and qualified mortgage insurance premiums you could not deduct on Schedule A because it is more than the limit on home mortgage interest or qualified mortgage insurance premiums. Do not include interest on a loan that did not benefit the dwelling unit (as explained in the line 2a instructions).

Line 4d. You can deduct the amounts on lines 4a and 4b as rental expenses on Schedule E only to the extent they are not more than the amount on line 4d.

Line 6a. To find the rental portion of excess casualty and theft losses, use the Form 4684 you prepared for line 2c of this worksheet.

A.	Enter the amount from Form 4684, line 10	
B.	Enter the rental portion of line A	
C.	Enter the amount from line 2c of this worksheet	
D.	Subtract line C from line B. Enter the result here and on line 6a of this worksheet	

Allocating the limited deduction. If you cannot deduct all of the amount on line 4c or 6c this year, you can allocate the allowable deduction in any way you wish among the expenses included on line 4c or 6c. Enter the amount you allocate to each expense on the appropriate line of Schedule E, Part I.

Line 6d. You can deduct the amounts on lines 6a and 6b as rental expenses on Schedule E only to the extent they are not more than the amount on line 6d.

Return. If you are not allowed to make the correction on an amended return, you can change your accounting method to claim the correct amount of depreciation. See *Changing your accounting method*, later.

Filing an amended return. You can file an amended return to correct the amount of depreciation claimed for any property in any of the following situations.

- You claimed the incorrect amount because of a mathematical error made in any year.
- You claimed the incorrect amount because of a posting error made in any year.
- You have not adopted a method of accounting for the property.

If an amended return is allowed, you must file it by the later of the following dates.

- 3 years from the date you filed your original return for the year in which you did not deduct the correct amount. (A return filed early is considered filed on the due date.)
- 2 years from the time you paid your tax for that year.

Changing your accounting method. To change your accounting method, you must file Form 3115, Application for Change in Accounting Method, to get the consent of the IRS. In some instances, that consent is automatic. For more information, see *Changing Your Accounting Method* in chapter 1 of Publication 946.

What Property Can be Depreciated

You can depreciate your property if it meets all the following requirements.

- You own the property.
- You use the property in your business or income-producing activity (such as rental property).
- The property has a determinable useful life.
- The property is expected to last more than 1 year.
- The property is not excepted property (such as property placed in service and disposed of in the same year and section 197 intangibles).

Property having a determinable useful life. To be depreciable, your property must have a determinable useful life. This means that it must be something that wears out, decays, gets used up, becomes obsolete, or loses its value from natural causes.

Land. You can never depreciate the cost of land because land does not wear out, become obsolete, or get used up. The costs of clearing, grading, planting, and landscaping are usually all part of the cost of land and cannot be depreciated.

Property you own. To claim depreciation, you usually must be the owner of the property. You are considered as owning property even if it is subject to a debt.

Rented property. Generally, if you pay rent on property, you cannot depreciate that property. Usually, only the owner can depreciate it. If you make permanent improvements to the property, you may be able to depreciate the improvements. See *Additions or improvements to property*, later, under *MACRS*.

Cooperative apartments. If you are a tenant-stockholder in a cooperative housing corporation and rent your cooperative apartment to others, you can deduct depreciation for your stock in the corporation.

Figure your depreciation deduction as follows.

1. Figure the depreciation for all the depreciable real property owned by the corporation. (Depreciation methods are discussed later.) If you bought your cooperative stock after its first offering, figure the depreciable basis of this property as follows.

    a. Multiply your cost per share by the total number of outstanding shares.

    b. Add to the amount figured in (a) any mortgage debt on the property on the date you bought the stock.

    c. Subtract from the amount figured in (b) any mortgage debt that is not for the depreciable real property, such as the part for the land.

2. Subtract from the amount figured in (1) any depreciation for space owned by the corporation that can be rented but cannot be lived in by tenant-stockholders.

3. Divide the number of your shares of stock by the total number of shares outstanding, including any shares held by the corporation.

4. Multiply the result of (2) by the percentage you figured in (3). This is your depreciation on the stock.

Your depreciation deduction for the year cannot be more than the part of your adjusted basis (defined later under *MACRS*) in the stock of the corporation that is allocable to your rental property.

See *Cooperative apartments* under *What Property Can Be Depreciated?* in chapter 1 of Publication 946 for more information.

No deduction greater than basis. The total of all your yearly depreciation deductions cannot be more than the cost or other basis of the property. For this purpose, your yearly depreciation deductions include any depreciation that you were allowed to claim, even if you did not claim it.

Depreciation Methods

There are three ways to figure depreciation. The depreciation method you use depends on the type of property and when it was placed in service. For property used in rental activities you use one of the following.

- MACRS (Modified Accelerated Cost Recovery System) for property placed in service after 1986.

- ACRS (Accelerated Cost Recovery System) for property placed in service after 1980 but before 1987.
- Useful lives and either straight line or an accelerated method of depreciation, such as the declining balance method, for property placed in service before 1981.

> **!** *This publication discusses MACRS only. If you need information about depreciating property placed in service before 1987, see Publication 534.*

If you placed property in service before 2007, continue to use the same method of figuring depreciation that you used in the past.

Section 179 deduction. You cannot claim the section 179 deduction for property held to produce rental income. See chapter 2 of Publication 946.

Alternative minimum tax. If you use accelerated depreciation, you may have to file Form 6251, Alternative Minimum Tax—Individuals. Accelerated depreciation can be determined under MACRS, ACRS, and any other method that allows you to deduct more depreciation than you could deduct using a straight line method.

Special Depreciation Allowance

You can take a special depreciation allowance (in addition to your regular MACRS depreciation deduction) for qualified Gulf Opportunity Zone (GO Zone) property you placed in service in 2007. The allowance is 50% of the property's depreciable basis. You figure the special depreciation allowance before you figure your regular MACRS deduction.

Choosing not to use the special allowance. If you want to take only the regular MACRS depreciation deduction, you must elect out of the special allowance. The election must be made separately for each class of property that has qualifying property. To make the election, attach a statement to your return indicating that you are electing out of the special depreciation allowance under IRC 1400N(d)(2)(B)(iv) and the class(es) of property for which you are making the election.

Qualified Gulf Opportunity Zone Property

Your property is qualified GO Zone property if it meets the following requirements.

1. It is one of the following types of property.

    a. Property depreciated under MACRS with a recovery period of 20 years or less.

    b. Water utility property.

    c. Certain computer software.

    d. Qualified leasehold improvement property.

    e. Certain nonresidential real property and residential rental property.

2. It meets the tests explained next under *Other tests to be met*.

3. It is not excepted property explained later under *Excepted property*.

Other tests to be met. To be qualified GO Zone property, the property must meet all of the following tests.

- Acquisition date test.
- Placed-in-service date test.
- Substantial use test.
- Original use test.

Acquisition date test. You must have acquired the property by purchase after August 27, 2005, with no binding written contract for the acquisition in effect before August 28, 2005.

Placed-in-service date test. The property must be placed in service for use in your trade or business or for the production of income before January 1, 2008 (January 1, 2009, in the case of qualifying nonresidential real property and residential rental property).

Substantial use test. Substantially all (80 percent or more) of the use of the property must be in the GO Zone and in the active conduct of your trade or business in the GO Zone.

Original use test. The original use of the property in the GO Zone must have begun with you after August 27, 2005.

Used property can be qualified GO Zone property if it has not previously been used within the GO Zone. Also, additional capital expenditures you incurred after August 27, 2005, to recondition or rebuild your property meet the original use test if the original use of the property in the GO Zone began with you.

If you sold property you placed in service after August 27, 2005, and you leased it back within 3 months after you originally placed the property in service, the lessor is considered to be the original user of the property.

Excepted property. Qualified GO Zone property does not include any of the following.

- Property required to be depreciated using the Alternative Depreciation System (ADS).
- Property any portion of which is financed with the proceeds of a tax-exempt obligation under section 103 of the Internal Revenue Code.
- Any qualified revitalization building for which you have elected to claim a commercial revitalization deduction for qualified revitalization expenditures.
- Any property used in connection with any private or commercial golf course, country club, massage parlor, hot tub facility, suntan facility, or any store, the principal business of which is the sale of alcoholic beverages for consumption off premises.
- Any gambling or animal racing property.
- Property for which you elected not to claim any special depreciation allowance.

More information. For more information about the special depreciation allowance, see Publication 946.

MACRS

Most business and investment property placed in service after 1986 is depreciated using MACRS.

MACRS consists of two systems that determine how you depreciate your property—the General Depreciation System (GDS) and the Alternative Depreciation System (ADS). GDS is used to figure your depreciation deduction for property used in most rental activities, unless you elect ADS.

To figure your MACRS deduction, you need to know the following information about your property:

- Its recovery period,
- Its placed-in-service date, and
- Its depreciable basis.

Personal home changed to rental use. You must use MACRS to figure the depreciation on property used as your home and changed to rental property in 2007.

Excluded property. You cannot use MACRS for certain personal property placed in service in your rental property in 2007 if it had been previously placed in service before MACRS became effective. Generally, personal property is excluded from MACRS if you (or a person related to you) owned or used it in 1986 or if your tenant is a person (or someone related to the person) who owned or used it in 1986. However, the property is not excluded if your 2007 deduction under MACRS (using a half-year convention) is less than the deduction you would have under ACRS. See *What Method Can You Use To Depreciate Your Property?* in chapter 1 of Publication 946 for more information.

Recovery Periods Under GDS

Each item of property that can be depreciated is assigned to a property class. The recovery period of the property depends on the class the property is in. Under GDS, the recovery period of an asset is generally the same as its property class. The property classes under GDS are:

- 3-year property,
- 5-year property,
- 7-year property,
- 10-year property,
- 15-year property,
- 20-year property,
- Nonresidential real property, and
- Residential rental property.

The class to which property is assigned is determined by its class life. Class lives and recovery periods for most assets are listed in *Appendix B* in Publication 946.

Under GDS, property that you placed in service during 2007 in your rental activities generally falls into one of the following classes. Also see Table 2.

- *5-year property.* This class includes computers and peripheral equipment, office machinery (typewriters, calculators, copiers, etc.), automobiles, and light trucks.

  This class also includes appliances, carpeting, furniture, etc., used in a residential rental real estate activity.

  Depreciation on automobiles, certain computers, and cellular telephones is limited. See chapter 5 of Publication 946.

- *7-year property.* This class includes office furniture and equipment (desks, files, etc.). This class also includes any property that does not have a class life and that has not been designated by law as being in any other class.

- *15-year property.* This class includes roads and shrubbery (if depreciable).

- *Residential rental property.* This class includes any real property that is a rental building or structure (including a mobile home) for which 80% or more of the gross rental income for the tax year is from dwelling units. It does not include a unit in a hotel, motel, inn, or other establishment where more than half of the units are used on a transient basis. If you live in any part of the building or structure, the gross rental income includes the fair rental value of the part you live in. The recovery period for residential rental property is 27.5 years.

> The other property classes do not generally apply to property used in rental activities. These classes are not discussed in this publication. See Publication 946 for more information.

Qualified Indian reservation property. Shorter recovery periods are provided under MACRS for qualified Indian reservation property placed in service on Indian reservations before 2008. For more information, see chapter 4 of Publication 946.

Additions or improvements to property. Treat depreciable additions or improvements you make to any property as separate property items for depreciation purposes. The recovery period for an addition or improvement to property begins on the later of:

- The date the addition or improvement is placed in service, or
- The date the property to which the addition or improvement was made is placed in service.

The property class and recovery period of the addition or improvement is the one that would apply to the original property if it were placed in service at the same time as the addition or improvement.

Example. You own a residential rental house that you have been renting since 1986 and that you are depreciating under ACRS. You put an addition onto the house and placed it in service in 2007. You must use MACRS for the

Table 2. MACRS Recovery Periods for Property Used in Rental Activities

Type of Property	MACRS Recovery Period	
	General Depreciation System	Alternative Depreciation System
Computers and their peripheral equipment	5 years	5 years

Office machinery, such as:
    Typewriters
    Calculators
    Copiers . . . .
	5 years	6 years

Automobiles	5 years	5 years
Light trucks	5 years	5 years

Appliances, such as:
    Stoves
    Refrigerators . . . .
	5 years	9 years

Carpets	5 years	9 years
Furniture used in rental property	5 years	9 years

Office furniture and equipment, such as:
    Desks
    Files . . . .
	7 years	10 years

Any property that does not have a class life and that has not been designated by law as being in any other class	7 years	12 years
Roads	15 years	20 years
Shrubbery	15 years	20 years
Fences	15 years	20 years
Residential rental property (buildings or structures) and structural components such as furnaces, waterpipes, venting, etc.	27.5 years	40 years
Additions and improvements, such as a new roof	The same recovery period as that of the property to which the addition or improvement is made, determined as if the property were placed in service at the same time as the addition or improvement.	

addition. Under GDS, the addition is depreciated as residential rental property over 27.5 years.

Placed-in-Service Date

You can begin to depreciate property when you place it in service in your trade or business or for the production of income. Property is considered placed in service in a rental activity when it is ready and available for a specific use in that activity.

Example 1. On November 22 of last year, you purchased a dishwasher for your rental property. The appliance was delivered on December 7, but was not installed and ready for use until January 3 of this year. Because the dishwasher was not ready for use last year, it is not considered placed in service until this year.

If the appliance had been ready for use when it was delivered in December of last year, it would have been considered placed in service in December, even if it was not actually used until this year.

Example 2. On April 6, you purchased a house to use as residential rental property. You made extensive repairs to the house and had it ready for rent on July 5. You began to advertise the house for rent in July and actually rented it beginning September 1. The house is considered placed in service in July when it was ready

and available for rent. You can begin to depreciate the house in July.

Example 3. You moved from your home in July. During August and September you made several repairs to the house. On October 1, you listed the property for rent with a real estate company, which rented it on December 1. The property is considered placed in service on October 1, the date when it was available for rent.

Depreciable Basis

The depreciable basis of property used in a rental activity is generally its adjusted basis when you place it in service in that activity. This is its cost or other basis when you acquired it, adjusted for certain items occurring before you place it in service in the rental activity.

If you depreciate your property under MACRS, you may also have to reduce your basis by certain deductions and credits with respect to the property.

Basis and adjusted basis are explained in the following discussions.

⚠️ **CAUTION** *If you used the property for personal purposes before changing it to rental use, its depreciable basis is the lesser of its adjusted basis or its fair market value when you change it to rental use. See Basis of Property Changed to Rental Use, later.*

Cost Basis

The basis of property you buy is usually its cost. The cost is the amount you pay for it in cash, in debt obligation, in other property, or in services. Your cost also includes amounts you pay for:

- Sales tax charged on the purchase (but see *Exception* below),
- Freight charges to obtain the property, and
- Installation and testing charges.

Exception. You can elect to deduct state and local general sales taxes instead of state and local income taxes as an itemized deduction on Schedule A (Form 1040). If you make that choice, you cannot include those sales taxes as part of your cost basis.

Loans with low or no interest. If you buy property on any time-payment plan that charges little or no interest, the basis of your property is your stated purchase price, less the amount considered to be unstated interest. See *Unstated Interest and Original Issue Discount (OID)* in Publication 537, Installment Sales.

Real property. If you buy real property, such as a building and land, certain fees and other expenses you pay are part of your cost basis in the property.

Real estate taxes. If you buy real property and agree to pay real estate taxes on it that were owed by the seller and the seller did not reimburse you, the taxes you pay are treated as part of your basis in the property. You cannot deduct them as taxes paid.

If you reimburse the seller for real estate taxes the seller paid for you, you can usually deduct that amount. Do not include that amount in your basis in the property.

Settlement fees and other costs. Settlement fees and closing costs that are for buying the property are part of your basis in the property. These include:

- Abstract fees,
- Charges for installing utility services,
- Legal fees,
- Recording fees,
- Surveys,
- Transfer taxes,
- Title insurance, and
- Any amounts the seller owes that you agree to pay, such as back taxes or interest, recording or mortgage fees, charges for improvements or repairs, and sales commissions.

Some settlement fees and closing costs you cannot include in your basis in the property are:

1. Fire insurance premiums,
2. Rent or other charges relating to occupancy of the property before closing, and
3. Charges connected with getting or refinancing a loan, such as:
   a. Points (discount points, loan origination fees),

b. Mortgage insurance premiums,

c. Loan assumption fees,

d. Cost of a credit report, and

e. Fees for an appraisal required by a lender.

Also, do not include amounts placed in escrow for the future payment of items such as taxes and insurance.

Assumption of a mortgage. If you buy property and become liable for an existing mortgage on the property, your basis is the amount you pay for the property plus the amount that still must be paid on the mortgage.

Example. You buy a building for $60,000 cash and assume a mortgage of $240,000 on it. Your basis is $300,000.

Land and buildings. If you buy buildings and your cost includes the cost of the land on which they stand, you must divide the cost between the land and the buildings to figure the basis for depreciation of the buildings. The part of the cost that you allocate to each asset is the ratio of the fair market value of that asset to the fair market value of the whole property at the time you buy it.

If you are not certain of the fair market values of the land and the buildings, you can divide the cost between them based on their assessed values for real estate tax purposes.

Example. You buy a house and land for $100,000. The purchase contract does not specify how much of the purchase price is for the house and how much is for the land.

The latest real estate tax assessment on the property was based on an assessed value of $80,000, of which $68,000 is for the house and $12,000 is for the land.

You can allocate 85% ($68,000 ÷ $80,000) of the purchase price to the house and 15% ($12,000 ÷ $80,000) of the purchase price to the land.

Your basis in the house is $85,000 (85% of $100,000) and your basis in the land is $15,000 (15% of $100,000).

Basis Other Than Cost

There are many times when you cannot use cost as a basis. You cannot use cost as a basis for property that you received:

* In return for services you performed,

* In an exchange for other property,

* As a gift,

* From your spouse, or from your former spouse as the result of a divorce, or

* As an inheritance.

If you received property in one of these ways, see Publication 551 for information on how to figure your basis.

Adjusted Basis

Before you can figure allowable depreciation, you may have to make certain adjustments (increases and decreases) to the basis of the property. The result of these adjustments to the basis is the adjusted basis.

Increases to basis. You must increase the basis of any property by the cost of all items properly added to a capital account. This includes:

* The cost of any additions or improvements having a useful life of more than one year,

* Amounts spent after a casualty to restore the damaged property,

* The cost of extending utility service lines to the property, and

* Legal fees, such as the cost of defending and perfecting title.

Additions or improvements. Add to the basis of your property the amount an addition or improvement actually cost you, including any amount you borrowed to make the addition or improvement. This includes all direct costs, such as material and labor, but not your own labor. It also includes all expenses related to the addition or improvement.

For example, if you had an architect draw up plans for remodeling your property, the architect's fee is a part of the cost of the remodeling. Or, if you had your lot surveyed to put up a fence, the cost of the survey is a part of the cost of the fence.

Keep separate accounts for depreciable additions or improvements made after you place the property in service in your rental activity. For information on depreciating additions or improvements, see *Additions or improvements to property*, earlier, under *Recovery Periods Under GDS*.

 The cost of landscaping improvements is usually treated as an addition to the basis of the land, which is not depreciable. See What Property Can Be Depreciated, *earlier.*

Assessments for local improvements. Assessments for items which tend to increase the value of property, such as streets and sidewalks, must be added to the basis of the property. For example, if your city installs curbing on the street in front of your house, and assesses you and your neighbors for the cost of curbing, you must add the assessment to the basis of your property. Also add the cost of legal fees paid to obtain a decrease in an assessment levied against property to pay for local improvements. You cannot deduct these items as taxes or depreciate them.

Assessments for maintenance or repair or meeting interest charges are deductible as taxes. Do not add them to your basis in the property.

Deducting vs. capitalizing costs. You cannot add to your basis costs that are deductible as current expenses. However, there are certain costs you can choose either to deduct or to capitalize. If you capitalize these costs, include them in your basis. If you deduct them, do not include them in your basis.

The costs you may be able to choose to deduct or to capitalize include carrying charges, such as interest and taxes, that you must pay to own property.

For more information about deducting or capitalizing costs, see chapter 7 in Publication 535.

Decreases to basis. You must decrease the basis of your property by any items that represent a return of your cost. These include:

* The amount of any insurance or other payment you receive as the result of a casualty or theft loss,

* Any deductible casualty loss not covered by insurance,

* Any amount you receive for granting an easement,

* Any residential energy credit you were allowed before 1986, or after 2005, if you added the cost of the energy items to the basis of your home, and

* The amount of depreciation you could have deducted on your tax returns under the method of depreciation you selected. If you took less depreciation than you could have under the method you selected, you must decrease the basis by the amount you could have taken under that method.

If you deducted more depreciation than you should have, you must decrease your basis by the amount you should have deducted, plus the part of the excess you deducted that actually lowered your tax liability for any year.

Basis of Property Changed to Rental Use

When you change property you held for personal use to rental use (for example, you rent your former home), you figure the basis for depreciation using the lesser of fair market value or adjusted basis.

Fair market value. This is the price at which the property would change hands between a buyer and a seller, neither having to buy or sell, and both having reasonable knowledge of all the relevant facts. Sales of similar property, on or about the same date, may be helpful in figuring the fair market value of the property.

Figuring the basis. The basis for depreciation is the lesser of:

* The fair market value of the property on the date you changed it to rental use, or

* Your adjusted basis on the date of the change—that is, your original cost or other basis of the property, plus the cost of permanent additions or improvements since you acquired it, minus deductions for any casualty or theft losses claimed on earlier years' income tax returns and other decreases to basis.

Example. Several years ago you built your home for $140,000 on a lot that cost you $14,000. Before changing the property to rental use last year, you added $28,000 of permanent improvements to the house and claimed a

$3,500 deduction for a casualty loss to the house. Because land is not depreciable, you can only include the cost of the house when figuring the basis for depreciation.

The adjusted basis of the house at the time of the change in use was $164,500 ($140,000 + $28,000 − $3,500).

On the date of the change in use, your property had a fair market value of $168,000, of which $21,000 was for the land and $147,000 was for the house.

The basis for depreciation on the house is the fair market value at the date of the change ($147,000), because it is less than your adjusted basis ($164,500).

MACRS Depreciation Under GDS

You can figure your MACRS depreciation deduction under GDS in one of two ways. The deduction is substantially the same both ways. (The difference, if any, is slight.) You can either:

- Actually compute the deduction using the depreciation method and convention that apply over the recovery period of the property, or

- Use the percentage from the optional MACRS tables, shown later.

If you actually compute the deduction, the depreciation method you use depends on the class of the property.

5-, 7-, or 15-year property. For property in the 5- or 7-year class, use the 200% declining balance method and a half-year convention. However, in limited cases you must use the mid-quarter convention, if it applies. These conventions are explained later. For property in the 15-year class, use the 150% declining balance method and a half-year convention.

You can also choose to use the 150% declining balance method for property in the 5- or 7-year class. The choice to use the 150% method for one item in a class of property applies to all property in that class that is placed in service during the tax year of the election. You make this election on Form 4562. In Part III, column (f), enter "150 DB."

If you use either the 200% or 150% declining balance method, you figure your deduction using the straight line method in the first tax year that the straight line method gives you an equal or larger deduction.

You can also choose to use the straight line method with a half-year or mid-quarter convention for 5-, 7-, or 15-year property. The choice to use the straight line method for one item in a class of property applies to all property in that class that is placed in service during the tax year of the election. You elect the straight line method on Form 4562. In Part III, column (f), enter "S/L." Once you make this election, you cannot change to another method.

Residential rental property. You must use the straight line method and a mid-month convention for residential rental property.

Declining Balance Method

To figure your MACRS deduction, first determine your declining balance rate from the table

on the next page. However, if you elect to use the 150% declining balance method for 5- or 7-year property, figure the declining balance rate by dividing 1.5 (150%) by the recovery period for the property.

In the first tax year, multiply the adjusted basis of the property by the declining balance rate and apply the appropriate convention to figure your depreciation. In later years (before the year you switch to the straight line method), use the following steps to figure your depreciation.

1. Reduce your adjusted basis by the depreciation allowable for the earlier years.

2. Multiply the new adjusted basis in (1) by the same rate used in earlier years.

See *Conventions*, later, for information on depreciation in the year you dispose of property.

Declining balance rates. The following table shows the declining balance rate that applies for each class of property and the first year for which the straight line method will give an equal or greater deduction. (The rates for 5- and 7-year property are based on the 200% declining balance method. The rate for 15-year property is based on the 150% declining balance method.)

Class	Declining Balance Rate	Year
5	40%	4th
7	28.57%	5th
15	10%	7th

Straight Line Method

To figure your MACRS deduction under the straight line method, you must apply a different depreciation rate to the adjusted basis of your property for each tax year in the recovery period.

In the first year, multiply the adjusted basis of the property by the straight line rate. You must figure the depreciation for the first year using the convention that applies. (See *Conventions*, later.)

Straight line rate. For any tax year, figure the straight line rate by dividing the number 1 by the years remaining in the recovery period at the beginning of the tax year. When figuring the number of years remaining, you must take into account the convention used in the first year. If the remaining recovery period at the beginning of the tax year is less than 1 year, the straight line rate for that tax year is 100%.

Example. You place in service property with a basis of $1,000 and a 5-year recovery period. The straight line rate is 20% (1 divided by 5) for the first tax year. After you apply the half-year convention, the first year rate is 10% (20% divided by 2). Depreciation for the first year is $100.

At the beginning of the second year, the remaining recovery period is 4½ years because of the half-year convention. The straight line rate for the second year is 22.22% (1 divided by 4.5).

To figure your depreciation deduction for the second year:

1. Subtract the depreciation taken in the first year ($100) from the basis of the property ($1,000), and

2. Multiply the remaining basis ($900) by 22.22%. The depreciation for the second year is $200.

Residential rental property. In the first year that you claim depreciation for residential rental property, you can only claim depreciation for the number of months the property is in use, and you must use the mid-month convention (explained under *Conventions*, next).

Conventions

Under MACRS, conventions establish when the recovery period begins and ends. The convention you use determines the number of months for which you can claim depreciation in the year you place property in service and in the year you dispose of the property.

Mid-month convention. A mid-month convention is used for all residential rental property and nonresidential real property. Under this convention, you treat all property placed in service, or disposed of, during any month as placed in service, or disposed of, at the midpoint of that month.

Mid-quarter convention. A mid-quarter convention must be used if the mid-month convention does not apply and the total depreciable basis of MACRS property placed in service in the last 3 months of a tax year (excluding nonresidential real property, residential rental property, and property placed in service and disposed of in the same year) is more than 40% of the total basis of all such property you place in service during the year.

Under this convention, you treat all property placed in service, or disposed of, during any quarter of a tax year as placed in service, or disposed of, at the midpoint of the quarter.

Example. During the tax year, Tom Martin purchased the following items to use in his rental property. He elects not to claim the special depreciation allowance, discussed earlier.

- A dishwasher for $400 that he placed in service in January.

- Used furniture for $100 that he placed in service in September.

- A refrigerator for $500 that he placed in service in October.

Tom uses the calendar year as his tax year. The total basis of all property placed in service that year is $1,000. The $500 basis of the refrigerator placed in service during the last 3 months of his tax year exceeds $400 (40% × $1,000). Tom must use the mid-quarter convention instead of the half-year convention for all three items.

Half-year convention. The half-year convention is used if neither the mid-quarter convention nor the mid-month convention applies. Under this convention, you treat all property placed in service, or disposed of, during a tax year as placed in service, or disposed of, at the midpoint of that tax year.

If this convention applies, you deduct a half-year of depreciation for the first year and the last year that you depreciate the property. You deduct a full year of depreciation for any other year during the recovery period.

Table 3. Optional MACRS Tables

Table 3-A. MACRS 5-Year Property

Year	Half-year convention	Mid-quarter convention			
		First quarter	Second quarter	Third quarter	Fourth quarter
1	20.00%	35.00%	25.00%	15.00%	5.00%
2	32.00	26.00	30.00	34.00	38.00
3	19.20	15.60	18.00	20.40	22.80
4	11.52	11.01	11.37	12.24	13.68
5	11.52	11.01	11.37	11.30	10.94
6	5.76	1.38	4.26	7.06	9.58

Table 3-B. MACRS 7-Year Property

Year	Half-year convention	Mid-quarter convention			
		First quarter	Second quarter	Third quarter	Fourth quarter
1	14.29%	25.00%	17.85%	10.71%	3.57%
2	24.49	21.43	23.47	25.51	27.55
3	17.49	15.31	16.76	18.22	19.68
4	12.49	10.93	11.97	13.02	14.06
5	8.93	8.75	8.87	9.30	10.04
6	8.92	8.74	8.87	8.85	8.73

Table 3-C. MACRS 15-Year Property

Year	Half-year convention	Mid-quarter convention			
		First quarter	Second quarter	Third quarter	Fourth quarter
1	5.00%	8.75%	6.25%	3.75%	1.25%
2	9.50	9.13	9.38	9.63	9.88
3	8.55	8.21	8.44	8.66	8.89
4	7.70	7.39	7.59	7.80	8.00
5	6.93	6.65	6.83	7.02	7.20
6	6.23	5.99	6.15	6.31	6.48

Table 3-D. Residential Rental Property (27.5-year)

	Use the row for the month of the taxable year placed in service.					
	Year 1	Year 2	Year 3	Year 4	Year 5	Year 6
Jan.	3.485%	3.636%	3.636%	3.636%	3.636%	3.636%
Feb.	3.182	3.636	3.636	3.636	3.636	3.636
March	2.879	3.636	3.636	3.636	3.636	3.636
Apr.	2.576	3.636	3.636	3.636	3.636	3.636
May	2.273	3.636	3.636	3.636	3.636	3.636
June	1.970	3.636	3.636	3.636	3.636	3.636
July	1.667	3.636	3.636	3.636	3.636	3.636
Aug.	1.364	3.636	3.636	3.636	3.636	3.636
Sept.	1.061	3.636	3.636	3.636	3.636	3.636
Oct.	0.758	3.636	3.636	3.636	3.636	3.636
Nov.	0.455	3.636	3.636	3.636	3.636	3.636
Dec.	0.152	3.636	3.636	3.636	3.636	3.636

Optional Tables

You can use the percentages in Table 3 to compute annual depreciation under MACRS. The tables show the percentages for the first 6 years. See *Appendix A* of Publication 946 for complete tables. The percentages in Tables 3-A, 3-B, and 3-C make the change from declining balance to straight line in the year that straight line will yield a larger deduction. See *Declining Balance Method*, earlier.

If you elect to use the straight line method for 5-, 7-, or 15-year property, or the 150% declining balance method for 5- or 7-year property, use the tables in *Appendix A* of Publication 946.

How to use the tables. The following section explains how to use the optional tables.

Figure the depreciation deduction by multiplying your unadjusted basis in the property by the percentage shown in the appropriate table. Your unadjusted basis is your depreciable basis without reduction for MACRS depreciation previously claimed.

Once you begin using an optional table to figure depreciation, you must continue to use it for the entire recovery period unless there is an adjustment to the basis of your property for a reason other than:

1. Depreciation allowed or allowable, or
2. An addition or improvement that is depreciated as a separate item of property.

If there is an adjustment for any reason other than (1) or (2) (for example, because of a deductible casualty loss) you can no longer use the table. For the year of the adjustment and for the remaining recovery period, figure depreciation using the property's adjusted basis at the end of the year and the appropriate depreciation method, as explained earlier under *MACRS Depreciation Under GDS*.

Tables 3-A, 3-B, and 3-C. The percentages in these tables take into account the half-year and mid-quarter conventions. Use Table 3-A for 5-year property, Table 3-B for 7-year property, and Table 3-C for 15-year property. Use the percentage in the second column (half-year convention) unless you must use the mid-quarter convention (explained earlier). If you must use the mid-quarter convention, use the column that corresponds to the calendar year quarter in which you placed the property in service.

Example 1. You purchased a stove and refrigerator and placed them in service in June. Your basis in the stove is $600 and your basis in the refrigerator is $1,000. Both are 5-year property. Using the half-year convention column in Table 3-A, you find the depreciation percentage for year 1 is 20%. For that year your depreciation deduction is $120 ($600 × .20) for the stove and $200 ($1,000 × .20) for the refrigerator.

For year 2, you find your depreciation percentage is 32%. That year's depreciation deduction will be $192 ($600 × .32) for the stove and $320 ($1,000 × .32) for the refrigerator.

Example 2. Assume the same facts as in *Example 1*, except you buy the refrigerator in October instead of June. You must use the mid-quarter convention to figure depreciation on the stove and refrigerator. The refrigerator was placed in service in the last 3 months of the tax year, and its basis ($1,000) is more than 40% of the total basis of all property placed in service during the year ($1,600 × .40 = $640).

Because you placed the refrigerator in service in October, you use the fourth quarter column of Table 3-A and find that the depreciation percentage for year 1 is 5%. Your depreciation deduction for the refrigerator is $50 ($1,000 × .05).

Because you placed the stove in service in June, you use the second quarter column of Table 3-A and find that the depreciation percentage for year 1 is 25%. For that year, your depreciation deduction for the stove is $150 ($600 × .25).

Table 3-D. Use this table for residential rental property. Find the row for the month that you placed the property in service. Use the percentages listed for that month to figure your depreciation deduction. The mid-month convention is taken into account in the percentages shown in the table.

Example. You purchased a single family rental house and placed it in service in February. Your basis in the house is $160,000. Using *Table 3-D*, you find that the percentage for property placed in service in February of year 1 is 3.182%. That year's depreciation deduction is $5,091 ($160,000 × .03182).

MACRS Depreciation Under ADS

If you choose, you can use the ADS method for most property. Under ADS, you use the straight line method of depreciation.

Table 2 shows the recovery periods for property used in rental activities that you depreciate under ADS.

See *Appendix B* in Publication 946 for other property. If your property is not listed, it is considered to have no class life. Under ADS, personal property with no class life is depreciated using a recovery period of 12 years.

Use the mid-month convention for residential rental property and nonresidential real property. For all other property, use the half-year or mid-quarter convention.

Election. For property placed in service during 2007 you choose to use ADS by entering the depreciation on Form 4562, Part III, line 20.

The election of ADS for one item in a class of property generally applies to all property in that class that is placed in service during the tax year of the election. However, the election applies on a property-by-property basis for residential rental property and nonresidential real property.

Once you choose to use ADS, you cannot change your election.

Casualties and Thefts

As a result of a casualty or theft, you may have a loss related to your property. You may be able to deduct the loss on your income tax return. For information on casualty and theft losses (business and nonbusiness), see Publication 547.

Casualty. Damage to, destruction of, or loss of property is a casualty if it results from an identifiable event that is sudden, unexpected, or unusual.

Theft. The unlawful taking and removing of your money or property with the intent to deprive you of it is a theft.

Gain from casualty or theft. When you have a casualty to, or theft of, your property and you receive money, including insurance, that is more than your adjusted basis in the property, you generally must report the gain. However, under certain circumstances, you may defer paying tax by choosing to postpone reporting the gain. To do this, you must generally buy replacement property within 2 years after the close of the first tax year in which any part of your gain is realized. The cost of the replacement property must be equal to or more than the net insurance or other payment you received. For more information, see Publication 547.

How to report. If you had a casualty or theft that involved property used in your rental activity, you figure the net gain or loss in Section B of Form 4684, Casualties and Thefts. Also, you may have to report the net gain or loss from Form 4684 on Form 4797, Sales of Business Property. (Follow the instructions for Form 4684.)

Limits on Rental Losses

Rental real estate activities are generally considered passive activities, and the amount of loss you can deduct is limited. Generally, you cannot deduct losses from rental real estate activities unless you have income from other passive activities. However, you may be able to deduct rental losses without regard to whether you have income from other passive activities if you "materially" or "actively" participated in your rental activity. See *Passive Activity Limits*, later.

Losses from passive activities are first subject to the at-risk rules. At-risk rules limit the amount of deductible losses from holding most real property placed in service after 1986.

Exception. If your rental losses are less than $25,000, and you actively participated in the rental activity, the passive activity limits probably do not apply to you. See *Losses From Rental Real Estate Activities*, later.

Property used as a home. If you used the rental property as a home during the year, the passive activity rules do not apply to that home. Instead, you must follow the rules explained under *Personal Use of Dwelling Unit (Including Vacation Home)*, earlier.

At-Risk Rules

The at-risk rules place a limit on the amount you can deduct as losses from activities often described as tax shelters. Losses from holding real property (other than mineral property) placed in service before 1987 are not subject to the at-risk rules.

Generally, any loss from an activity subject to the at-risk rules is allowed only to the extent of the total amount you have at risk in the activity at the end of the tax year. You are considered at risk in an activity to the extent of cash and the adjusted basis of other property you contributed to the activity and certain amounts borrowed for use in the activity. See Publication 925 for more information.

Passive Activity Limits

In general, all rental activities (except those meeting the exception for real estate professionals, below) are passive activities. For this purpose, a rental activity is an activity from which you receive income mainly for the use of tangible property, rather than for services.

Limits on passive activity deductions and credits. Deductions for losses from passive activities are limited. You generally cannot offset income, other than passive income, with losses from passive activities. Nor can you offset taxes on income, other than passive income, with

credits resulting from passive activities. Any excess loss or credit is carried forward to the next tax year.

For a detailed discussion of these rules, see Publication 925.

You may have to complete Form 8582 to figure the amount of any passive activity loss for the current tax year for all activities and the amount of the passive activity loss allowed on your tax return. See *Form 8582 not required* under *Losses From Rental Real Estate Activities*, later, to determine whether you have to complete Form 8582.

Exception for Real Estate Professionals

Rental activities in which you materially participated during the year are not passive activities if, for that year, you were a real estate professional. Losses from these activities are not limited by the passive activity rules.

For this purpose, each interest you have in a rental real estate activity is a separate activity, unless you choose to treat all interests in rental real estate activities as one activity.

If you were a real estate professional for 2007, complete line 43 of Schedule E (Form 1040).

Real estate professional. You qualified as a real estate professional for the tax year if you met both of the following requirements.

- More than half of the personal services you performed in all trades or businesses during the tax year were performed in real property trades or businesses in which you materially participated.

- You performed more than 750 hours of services during the tax year in real property trades or businesses in which you materially participated.

Do not count personal services you performed as an employee in real property trades or businesses unless you were a 5% owner of your employer. You were a 5% owner if you owned (or are considered to have owned) more than 5% of your employer's outstanding stock, or capital or profits interest.

If you file a joint return, do not count your spouse's personal services to determine whether you met the preceding requirements. However, you can count your spouse's participation in an activity in determining if you materially participated.

Real property trades or businesses. A real property trade or business is a trade or business that does any of the following with real property.

- Develops or redevelops it.
- Constructs or reconstructs it.
- Acquires it.
- Converts it.
- Rents or leases it.
- Operates or manages it.
- Brokers it.

Material participation. Generally, you materially participated in an activity for the tax year if you were involved in its operations on a regular, continuous, and substantial basis during the year. For more information, see Publication 925.

Participating spouse. If you are married, determine whether you materially participated in an activity by also counting any participation in the activity by your spouse during the year. Do this even if your spouse owns no interest in the activity or files a separate return for the year.

Choice to treat all interests as one activity. If you were a real estate professional and had more than one rental real estate interest during the year, you can choose to treat all the interests as one activity. You can make this choice for any year that you qualify as a real estate professional. If you forgo making the choice for one year, you can still make it for a later year.

If you make the choice, it is binding for the tax year you make it and for any later year that you are a real estate professional. This is true even if you are not a real estate professional in any intervening year. (For that year, the exception for real estate professionals will not apply in determining whether your activity is subject to the passive activity rules.)

See the instructions for Schedule E (Form 1040) for information about making this choice.

Losses From Rental Real Estate Activities

If you or your spouse actively participated in a passive rental real estate activity, you can deduct up to $25,000 of loss from the activity from your nonpassive income. This special allowance is an exception to the general rule disallowing losses in excess of income from passive activities. Similarly, you can offset credits from the activity against the tax on up to $25,000 of nonpassive income after taking into account any losses allowed under this exception.

If you are married, filing a separate return, and lived apart from your spouse for the entire tax year, your special allowance cannot be more than $12,500. If you lived with your spouse at any time during the year and are filing a separate return, you cannot use the special allowance to reduce your nonpassive income or tax on nonpassive income.

The maximum amount of the special allowance is reduced if your modified adjusted gross income is more than $100,000 ($50,000 if married filing separately).

Example. Jane is single and has $40,000 in wages, $2,000 of passive income from a limited partnership, and $3,500 of passive loss from a rental real estate activity in which she actively participated. $2,000 of Jane's $3,500 loss offsets her passive income. The remaining $1,500 loss can be deducted from her $40,000 wages.

Active participation. You actively participated in a rental real estate activity if you (and your spouse) owned at least 10% of the rental property and you made management decisions in a significant and *bona fide* sense. Management decisions include approving new tenants, deciding on rental terms, approving expenditures, and similar decisions.

Example. Mike is single and had the following income and losses during the tax year:

Salary	$42,300
Dividends	300
Interest	1,400
Rental loss	(4,000)

The rental loss resulted from the rental of a house Mike owned. Mike had advertised and rented the house to the current tenant himself. He also collected the rents, which usually came by mail. All repairs were either done or contracted out by Mike.

Even though the rental loss is a loss from a passive activity, because Mike actively participated in the rental property management, he can use the entire $4,000 loss to offset his other income.

Maximum special allowance. If your modified adjusted gross income is $100,000 or less ($50,000 or less if married filing separately), you can deduct your loss up to $25,000 ($12,500 if married filing separately). If your modified adjusted gross income is more than $100,000 (more than $50,000 if married filing separately), this special allowance is limited to 50% of the difference between $150,000 ($75,000 if married filing separately) and your modified adjusted gross income. If your modified adjusted gross income is $150,000 or more ($75,000 or more if you are married filing separately), you generally cannot use the special allowance.

Modified adjusted gross income. This is your adjusted gross income from Form 1040, line 38, or Form 1040NR, line 36, figured without taking into account:

1. Taxable social security or equivalent tier 1 railroad retirement benefits,

2. Deductible contributions to an IRA or certain other qualified retirement plans,

3. The exclusion allowed for qualified U.S. savings bond interest used to pay higher educational expenses,

4. The exclusion allowed for employer-provided adoption benefits,

5. Any passive activity income or loss included on Form 8582,

6. Any passive income or loss or any loss allowable by reason of the exception for real estate professionals discussed earlier,

7. Any overall loss from a publicly traded partnership (see *Publicly Traded Partnerships (PTPs)* in the instructions for Form 8582),

8. The deduction for one-half of self-employment tax,

9. The deduction allowed for interest on student loans, or

10. The deduction for qualified tuition and related expenses, or

11. The deduction for income attributable to domestic production activities (see the instructions for Form 8903).

Form 8582 not required. Do not complete Form 8582 if you meet all of the following conditions.

- Your only passive activities were rental real estate activities in which you actively participated.

- Your overall net loss from these activities is $25,000 or less ($12,500 or less if married filing separately).

- You do not have any prior year unallowed losses from any passive activities.

- If married filing separately, you lived apart from your spouse all year.

- You have no current or prior year unallowed credits from passive activities.

- Your modified adjusted gross income is $100,000 or less ($50,000 or less if married filing separately).

- You do not hold any interest in a rental real estate activity as a limited partner or as a beneficiary of an estate or a trust.

If you meet all of the conditions listed above, your rental real estate activities are not limited by the passive activity rules and you do not have to complete Form 8582. Enter each rental real estate loss from line 22 of Schedule E (Form 1040) on line 23 of Schedule E.

If you do not meet all of the conditions listed above, see the instructions for Form 8582 to find out if you must complete and attach that form to your tax return.

How To Report Rental Income and Expenses

If you rent buildings, rooms, or apartments, and provide only heat and light, trash collection, etc., you normally report your rental income and expenses on Schedule E (Form 1040), Part I. However, do not use that schedule to report a not-for-profit activity. See *Not Rented For Profit*, earlier.

If you provide significant services that are primarily for your tenant's convenience, such as regular cleaning, changing linen, or maid service, you report your rental income and expenses on Schedule C (Form 1040), Profit or Loss From Business, or Schedule C-EZ, Net Profit From Business. Significant services do not include the furnishing of heat and light, cleaning of public areas, trash collection, etc. For information, see Publication 334, Tax Guide for Small Business. You also may have to pay self-employment tax on your rental income. See chapter 10 in Publication 334.

Schedule E (Form 1040)

Use Schedule E (Form 1040), Part I, to report your rental income and expenses. List your total income, expenses, and depreciation for each rental property. Be sure to answer the question on line 2.

If you have more than three rental or royalty properties, complete and attach as many Schedules E as are needed to list the properties. Complete lines 1 and 2 for each property. However, fill in the "Totals" column on only one Schedule E. The figures in the "Totals" column on that Schedule E should be the combined totals of all Schedules E.

Page 2 of Schedule E is used to report income or loss from partnerships, S corporations, estates, trusts, and real estate mortgage investment conduits. If you need to use page 2 of Schedule E, use page 2 of the same Schedule E you used to enter the combined totals in Part I.

On Schedule E, page 1, line 20, enter the depreciation you are claiming. You must complete and attach Form 4562 for rental activities only if you are claiming:

- Depreciation on property placed in service during 2007,
- Depreciation on listed property (such as a car), regardless of when it was placed in service, or
- Any car expenses reported on a form other than Schedule C or C-EZ (Form 1040) or Form 2106 or Form 2106-EZ.

Otherwise, figure your depreciation on your own worksheet. You do not have to attach these computations to your return.

Illustrated Example

In January, Eileen Johnson bought a condominium apartment to live in. Instead of selling the house she had been living in, she decided to change it to rental property. Eileen selected a tenant and started renting the house on February 1. Eileen charges $750 a month for rent and collects it herself. Eileen received a $750 security deposit from her tenant. Because she plans to return it to her tenant at the end of the lease, she does not include it in her income. Her house expenses for the year are as follows:

Mortgage interest	$1,800
Fire insurance (1-year policy)	100
Miscellaneous repairs (after renting)	297
Real estate taxes imposed and paid	1,200

Eileen must divide the real estate taxes, mortgage interest, and fire insurance between the personal use of the property and the rental use of the property. She can deduct eleven-twelfths of these expenses as rental expenses. She can include the balance of the allowable taxes and mortgage interest on Schedule A (Form 1040) if she itemizes. She cannot deduct the balance of the fire insurance because it is a personal expense.

Eileen bought this house in 1982 for $35,000. Her property tax was based on assessed values of $10,000 for the land and $25,000 for the house. Before changing it to rental property, Eileen added several improvements to the house. She figures her adjusted basis as follows:

Improvements	Cost
House	$25,000
Remodeled kitchen	4,200
Recreation room	5,800
New roof	1,600
Patio and deck	2,400
Adjusted basis	$39,000

On February 1, when Eileen changed her house to rental property, the property had a fair market value of $152,000. Of this amount, $35,000 was for the land and $117,000 was for the house.

Because Eileen's adjusted basis is less than the fair market value on the date of the change, Eileen uses $39,000 as her basis for depreciation.

Because the house is residential rental property, she must use the straight line method of depreciation using either the GDS recovery period or the ADS recovery period. She chooses the GDS recovery period of 27.5 years.

She uses Table 3-D to find her depreciation percentage. Because she placed the property in service in February, she finds the percentage to be 3.182%.

On April 1, Eileen bought a new dishwasher for the rental property at a cost of $425. The dishwasher is personal property used in a rental real estate activity, which has a 5-year recovery period. She uses the percentage under "Half-year convention" in Table 3-A to figure her MACRS depreciation deduction for the dishwasher.

On May 1, Eileen paid $4,000 to have a furnace installed in the house. The furnace is residential rental property. Because she placed the property in service in May, she finds the percentage from Table 3-D to be 2.273%.

Eileen figures her net rental income or loss for the house as follows:

Total rental income received ($750 × 11)		$8,250
Minus: Expenses		
Mortgage interest ($1,800 × $11/_{12}$)	$1,650	
Fire insurance ($100 × $11/_{12}$)	92	
Miscellaneous repairs	297	
Real estate taxes ($1,200 × $11/_{12}$)	1,100	
Total expenses		3,139
Balance		$5,111
Minus: Depreciation		
House ($39,000 × 3.182%)	$1,241	
Dishwasher ($425 × 20%)	85	
Furnace ($4,000 × 2.273%)	91	
Total depreciation		1,417
Net rental income for house		$3,694

Eileen uses Schedule E (Form 1040), Part I, to report her rental income and expenses. She enters her income, expenses, and depreciation for the house in the column for Property A. She uses Form 4562 to figure and report her depreciation. Eileen's Schedule E (Form 1040) is shown next. Her Form 4562 is not shown. See Publication 946 for information on how to prepare Form 4562.

SCHEDULE E (Form 1040)	Supplemental Income and Loss	OMB No. 1545-0074
Department of the Treasury Internal Revenue Service (99)	(From rental real estate, royalties, partnerships, S corporations, estates, trusts, REMICs, etc.) ▶ Attach to Form 1040, 1040NR, or Form 1041. ▶ See Instructions for Schedule E (Form 1040).	2008 Attachment Sequence No. 13

Name(s) shown on return

Your social security number

Part I Income or Loss From Rental Real Estate and Royalties **Note.** If you are in the business of renting personal property, use **Schedule C or C-EZ** (see page E-3). If you are an individual, report farm rental income or loss from **Form 4835** on page 2, line 40.

1 List the type and address of each **rental real estate property:**

A ....

B ....

C ....

2 For each rental real estate property listed on line 1, did you or your family use it during the tax year for personal purposes for more than the greater of:
- 14 days **or**
- 10% of the total days rented at fair rental value?
(See page E-3)

	Yes	No
A		
B		
C		

Income:		Properties			Totals (Add columns A, B, and C)
		A	B	C	
3 Rents received	3				3
4 Royalties received	4				4
Expenses:					
5 Advertising	5				
6 Auto and travel (see page E-4)	6				
7 Cleaning and maintenance	7				
8 Commissions	8				
9 Insurance	9				
10 Legal and other professional fees	10				
11 Management fees	11				
12 Mortgage interest paid to banks, etc. (see page E-5)	12				12
13 Other interest	13				
14 Repairs	14				
15 Supplies	15				
16 Taxes	16				
17 Utilities	17				
18 Other (list) ▶	18				
19 Add lines 5 through 18	19				19
20 Depreciation expense or depletion (see page E-5)	20				20
21 Total expenses. Add lines 19 and 20	21				
22 Income or (loss) from rental real estate or royalty properties. Subtract line 21 from line 3 (rents) or line 4 (royalties). If the result is a (loss), see page E-5 to find out if you must file **Form 6198**	22				
23 Deductible rental real estate loss. **Caution.** Your rental real estate loss on line 22 may be limited. See page E-5 to find out if you must file **Form 8582.** Real estate professionals **must** complete line 43 on page 2	23	(	)(	)(	)

24	Income. Add positive amounts shown on line 22. **Do not** include any losses	24	
25	Losses. Add royalty losses from line 22 and rental real estate losses from line 23. Enter total losses here	25	( )
26	Total rental real estate and royalty income or (loss). Combine lines 24 and 25. Enter the result here. If Parts II, III, IV, and line 40 on page 2 do not apply to you, also enter this amount on Form 1040, line 17, or Form 1040NR, line 18. Otherwise, include this amount in the total on line 41 on page 2	26	

For Paperwork Reduction Act Notice, see page E-8 of the instructions.   Cat. No. 11344L   Schedule E (Form 1040) 2008

Name(s) shown on return. Do not enter name and social security number if shown on other side. | Your social security number

Caution. The IRS compares amounts reported on your tax return with amounts shown on Schedule(s) K-1.

Part II   Income or Loss From Partnerships and S Corporations   **Note.** If you report a loss from an at-risk activity for which **any** amount is **not** at risk, you **must** check the box in column (e) on line 28 and attach **Form 6198.** See page E-1.

27   Are you reporting any loss not allowed in a prior year due to the at-risk or basis limitations, a prior year unallowed loss from a passive activity (if that loss was not reported on Form 8582), or unreimbursed partnership expenses?   ☐ Yes   ☐ No
If you answered "Yes," see page E-7 before completing this section.

28	(a) Name	(b) Enter P for partnership; S for S corporation	(c) Check if foreign partnership	(d) Employer identification number	(e) Check if any amount is not at risk
A			☐		☐
B			☐		☐
C			☐		☐
D			☐		☐

	Passive Income and Loss		Nonpassive Income and Loss		
	(f) Passive loss allowed (attach Form 8582 if required)	(g) Passive income from Schedule K-1	(h) Nonpassive loss from Schedule K-1	(i) Section 179 expense deduction from Form 4562	(j) Nonpassive income from Schedule K-1
A					
B					
C					
D					
29a Totals					
b Totals					

30	Add columns (g) and (j) of line 29a	30	
31	Add columns (f), (h), and (i) of line 29b	31	( )
32	**Total partnership and S corporation income or (loss).** Combine lines 30 and 31. Enter the result here and include in the total on line 41 below.	32	

Part III   Income or Loss From Estates and Trusts

33	(a) Name	(b) Employer identification number
A		
B		

	Passive Income and Loss		Nonpassive Income and Loss	
	(c) Passive deduction or loss allowed (attach Form 8582 if required)	(d) Passive income from Schedule K-1	(e) Deduction or loss from Schedule K-1	(f) Other income from Schedule K-1
A				
B				
34a Totals				
b Totals				

35	Add columns (d) and (f) of line 34a	35	
36	Add columns (c) and (e) of line 34b	36	( )
37	**Total estate and trust income or (loss).** Combine lines 35 and 36. Enter the result here and include in the total on line 41 below	37	

Part IV   Income or Loss From Real Estate Mortgage Investment Conduits (REMICs)—Residual Holder

38	(a) Name	(b) Employer identification number	(c) Excess inclusion from Schedules Q, line 2c (see page E-7)	(d) Taxable income (net loss) from Schedules Q, line 1b	(e) Income from Schedules Q, line 3b

39	Combine columns (d) and (e) only. Enter the result here and include in the total on line 41 below	39	

Part V   Summary

40	Net farm rental income or (loss) from **Form 4835.** Also, complete line 42 below	40	
41	**Total income or (loss).** Combine lines 26, 32, 37, 39, and 40. Enter the result here and on Form 1040, line 17, or Form 1040NR, line 18 ▶	41	

42   **Reconciliation of farming and fishing income.** Enter your **gross** farming and fishing income reported on Form 4835, line 7; Schedule K-1 (Form 1065), box 14, code B; Schedule K-1 (Form 1120S), box 17, code T; and Schedule K-1 (Form 1041), line 14, code F (see page E-8) | **42** | |

43   **Reconciliation for real estate professionals.** If you were a real estate professional (see page E-2), enter the net income or (loss) you reported anywhere on Form 1040 or Form 1040NR from all rental real estate activities in which you materially participated under the passive activity loss rules . | **43** | |

How To Get Tax Help

You can get help with unresolved tax issues, order free publications and forms, ask tax questions, and get information from the IRS in several ways. By selecting the method that is best for you, you will have quick and easy access to tax help.

Contacting your Taxpayer Advocate. The Taxpayer Advocate Service (TAS) is an independent organization within the IRS whose employees assist taxpayers who are experiencing economic harm, who are seeking help in resolving tax problems that have not been resolved through normal channels, or who believe that an IRS system or procedure is not working as it should.

You can contact the TAS by calling the TAS toll-free case intake line at 1-877-777-4778 or TTY/TDD 1-800-829-4059 to see if you are eligible for assistance. You can also call or write to your local taxpayer advocate, whose phone number and address are listed in your local telephone directory and in Publication 1546, Taxpayer Advocate Service - Your Voice at the IRS. You can file Form 911, Request for Taxpayer Advocate Service Assistance (And Application for Taxpayer Assistance Order), or ask an IRS employee to complete it on your behalf. For more information, go to *www.irs.gov/advocate*.

Taxpayer Advocacy Panel (TAP). The TAP listens to taxpayers, identifies taxpayer issues, and makes suggestions for improving IRS services and customer satisfaction. If you have suggestions for improvements, contact the TAP, toll free at 1-888-912-1227 or go to *www.improveirs.org*.

Low Income Taxpayer Clinics (LITCs). LITCs are independent organizations that provide low income taxpayers with representation in federal tax controversies with the IRS for free or for a nominal charge. The clinics also provide tax education and outreach for taxpayers with limited English proficiency or who speak English as a second language. Publication 4134, Low Income Taxpayer Clinic List, provides information on clinics in your area. It is available at *www.irs.gov* or at your local IRS office.

Free tax services. To find out what services are available, get Publication 910, IRS Guide to Free Tax Services. It contains a list of free tax publications and describes other free tax information services, including tax education and assistance programs and a list of TeleTax topics.

Accessible versions of IRS published products are available on request in a variety of alternative formats for people with disabilities.

 Internet. You can access the IRS website at *www.irs.gov* 24 hours a day, 7 days a week to:

* E-file your return. Find out about commercial tax preparation and e-file services available free to eligible taxpayers.

* Check the status of your 2007 refund. Click on *Where's My Refund*. Wait at least 6 weeks from the date you filed your return (3 weeks if you filed electronically). Have your 2007 tax return available because you will need to know your social security number, your filing status, and the exact whole dollar amount of your refund.

* Download forms, instructions, and publications.

* Order IRS products online.

* Research your tax questions online.

* Search publications online by topic or keyword.

* View Internal Revenue Bulletins (IRBs) published in the last few years.

* Figure your withholding allowances using the withholding calculator online at *www.irs.gov/individuals*.

* Determine if Form 6251 must be filed using our Alternative Minimum Tax (AMT) Assistant.

* Sign up to receive local and national tax news by email.

* Get information on starting and operating a small business.

Phone. Many services are available by phone.

* *Ordering forms, instructions, and publications.* Call 1-800-829-3676 to order current-year forms, instructions, and publications, and prior-year forms and instructions. You should receive your order within 10 days.

* *Asking tax questions.* Call the IRS with your tax questions at 1-800-829-1040.

* *Solving problems.* You can get face-to-face help solving tax problems every business day in IRS Taxpayer Assistance Centers. An employee can explain IRS letters, request adjustments to your account, or help you set up a payment plan. Call your local Taxpayer Assistance Center for an appointment. To find the number, go to *www.irs.gov/localcontacts* or look in the phone book under *United States Government, Internal Revenue Service*.

* *TTY/TDD equipment.* If you have access to TTY/TDD equipment, call 1-800-829-4059 to ask tax questions or to order forms and publications.

* *TeleTax topics.* Call 1-800-829-4477 to listen to pre-recorded messages covering various tax topics.

* *Refund information.* To check the status of your 2007 refund, call 1-800-829-4477 and press 1 for automated refund information or call 1-800-829-1954. Be sure to wait at least 6 weeks from the date you filed your return (3 weeks if you filed electronically). Have your 2007 tax return available because you will need to know your social security number, your filing status, and the exact whole dollar amount of your refund.

Evaluating the quality of our telephone services. To ensure IRS representatives give accurate, courteous, and professional answers, we use several methods to evaluate the quality of our telephone services. One method is for a second IRS representative to listen in on or record random telephone calls. Another is to ask some callers to complete a short survey at the end of the call.

Walk-in. Many products and services are available on a walk-in basis.

* *Products.* You can walk in to many post offices, libraries, and IRS offices to pick up certain forms, instructions, and publications. Some IRS offices, libraries, grocery stores, copy centers, city and county government offices, credit unions, and office supply stores have a collection of products available to print from a CD or photocopy from reproducible proofs. Also, some IRS offices and libraries have the Internal Revenue Code, regulations, Internal Revenue Bulletins, and Cumulative Bulletins available for research purposes.

* *Services.* You can walk in to your local Taxpayer Assistance Center every business day for personal, face-to-face tax help. An employee can explain IRS letters, request adjustments to your tax account, or help you set up a payment plan. If you need to resolve a tax problem, have questions about how the tax law applies to your individual tax return, or you're more comfortable talking with someone in person, visit your local Taxpayer Assistance Center where you can spread out your records and talk with an IRS representative face-to-face. No appointment is necessary, but if you prefer, you can call your local Center and leave a message requesting an appointment to resolve a tax account issue. A representative will call you back within 2 business days to schedule an in-person appointment at your convenience. To find the number, go to *www.irs.gov/localcontacts* or look in the phone book under *United States Government, Internal Revenue Service*.

Mail. You can send your order for forms, instructions, and publications to the address below. You should receive a response within 10 days after your request is received.

National Distribution Center
P.O. Box 8903
Bloomington, IL 61702-8903

 CD/DVD for tax products. You can order Publication 1796, IRS Tax Products CD/DVD, and obtain:

* Current-year forms, instructions, and publications.

* Prior-year forms, instructions, and publications.

* Bonus: Historical Tax Products DVD - Ships with the final release.

* Tax Map: an electronic research tool and finding aid.

* Tax law frequently asked questions.

- Tax Topics from the IRS telephone response system.

- Fill-in, print, and save features for most tax forms.

- Internal Revenue Bulletins.

- Toll-free and email technical support.

- The CD which is released twice during the year.
  – The first release will ship the beginning of January 2008.
  – The final release will ship the beginning of March 2008.

Purchase the CD/DVD from National Technical Information Service (NTIS) at *www.irs.gov/cdorders* for $35 (no handling fee) or call 1-877-CDFORMS (1-877-233-6767) toll free to buy the CD/DVD for $35 (plus a $5 handling fee). Price is subject to change.

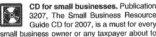 **CD for small businesses.** Publication 3207, The Small Business Resource Guide CD for 2007, is a must for every small business owner or any taxpayer about to start a business. This year's CD includes:

- Helpful information, such as how to prepare a business plan, find financing for your business, and much more.

- All the business tax forms, instructions, and publications needed to successfully manage a business.

- Tax law changes for 2007.

- Tax Map: an electronic research tool and finding aid.

- Web links to various government agencies, business associations, and IRS organizations.

- "Rate the Product" survey — your opportunity to suggest changes for future editions.

- A site map of the CD to help you navigate the pages of the CD with ease.

- An interactive "Teens in Biz" module that gives practical tips for teens about starting their own business, creating a business plan, and filing taxes.

An updated version of this CD is available each year in early April. You can get a free copy by calling 1-800-829-3676 or by visiting *www.irs.gov/smallbiz*.

Index

To help us develop a more useful index, please let us know if you have ideas for index entries. See "Comments and Suggestions" in the "Introduction" for the ways you can reach us.

Form **4797**

Department of the Treasury
Internal Revenue Service   (99)

Sales of Business Property

(Also Involuntary Conversions and Recapture Amounts
Under Sections 179 and 280F(b)(2))

▶ Attach to your tax return.▶ See separate instructions.

OMB No. 1545-0184

2007

Attachment
Sequence No. **27**

Name(s) shown on return

Identifying number

| 1 | Enter the gross proceeds from sales or exchanges reported to you for 2007 on Form(s) 1099-B or 1099-S (or substitute statement) that you are including on line 2, 10, or 20 (see instructions) | 1 | |

Part I **Sales or Exchanges of Property Used in a Trade or Business and Involuntary Conversions From Other Than Casualty or Theft—Most Property Held More Than 1 Year** (see instructions)

	(a) Description of property	(b) Date acquired (mo., day, yr.)	(c) Date sold (mo., day, yr.)	(d) Gross sales price	(e) Depreciation allowed or allowable since acquisition	(f) Cost or other basis, plus improvements and expense of sale	(g) Gain or (loss) Subtract (f) from the sum of (d) and (e)
2							

3	Gain, if any, from Form 4684, line 39	3	
4	Section 1231 gain from installment sales from Form 6252, line 26 or 37	4	
5	Section 1231 gain or (loss) from like-kind exchanges from Form 8824	5	
6	Gain, if any, from line 32, from other than casualty or theft	6	
7	Combine lines 2 through 6. Enter the gain or (loss) here and on the appropriate line as follows:	7	

Partnerships (except electing large partnerships) and S corporations. Report the gain or (loss) following the instructions for Form 1065, Schedule K, line 10, or Form 1120S, Schedule K, line 9. Skip lines 8, 9, 11, and 12 below.

Individuals, partners, S corporation shareholders, and all others. If line 7 is zero or a loss, enter the amount from line 7 on line 11 below and skip lines 8 and 9. If line 7 is a gain and you did not have any prior year section 1231 losses, or they were recaptured in an earlier year, enter the gain from line 7 as a long-term capital gain on the Schedule D filed with your return and skip lines 8, 9, 11, and 12 below.

| 8 | Nonrecaptured net section 1231 losses from prior years (see instructions) | 8 | |
| 9 | Subtract line 8 from line 7. If zero or less, enter -0-. If line 9 is zero, enter the gain from line 7 on line 12 below. If line 9 is more than zero, enter the amount from line 8 on line 12 below and enter the gain from line 9 as a long-term capital gain on the Schedule D filed with your return (see instructions) | 9 | |

Part II **Ordinary Gains and Losses** (see instructions)

10	Ordinary gains and losses not included on lines 11 through 16 (include property held 1 year or less):		

11	Loss, if any, from line 7	11	( )
12	Gain, if any, from line 7 or amount from line 8, if applicable	12	
13	Gain, if any, from line 31	13	
14	Net gain or (loss) from Form 4684, lines 31 and 38a	14	
15	Ordinary gain from installment sales from Form 6252, line 25 or 36	15	
16	Ordinary gain or (loss) from like-kind exchanges from Form 8824	16	
17	Combine lines 10 through 16	17	
18	For all except individual returns, enter the amount from line 17 on the appropriate line of your return and skip lines a and b below. For individual returns, complete lines a and b below:		
a	If the loss on line 11 includes a loss from Form 4684, line 35, column (b)(ii), enter that part of the loss here. Enter the part of the loss from income-producing property on Schedule A (Form 1040), line 28, and the part of the loss from property used as an employee on Schedule A (Form 1040), line 23. Identify as from "Form 4797, line 18a." See instructions	18a	
b	Redetermine the gain or (loss) on line 17 excluding the loss, if any, on line 18a. Enter here and on Form 1040, line 14	18b	

For Paperwork Reduction Act Notice, see separate instructions.

Cat. No. 13086I

Form **4797** (2007)

Part III Gain From Disposition of Property Under Sections 1245, 1250, 1252, 1254, and 1255 (see instructions)

19	(a) Description of section 1245, 1250, 1252, 1254, or 1255 property:	(b) Date acquired (mo., day, yr.)	(c) Date sold (mo., day, yr.)
A			
B			
C			
D			

	These columns relate to the properties on lines 19A through 19D. ▶		Property A	Property B	Property C	Property D
20	Gross sales price (Note: See line 1 before completing.)	20				
21	Cost or other basis plus expense of sale	21				
22	Depreciation (or depletion) allowed or allowable	22				
23	Adjusted basis. Subtract line 22 from line 21	23				
24	Total gain. Subtract line 23 from line 20	24				
25	**If section 1245 property:**					
a	Depreciation allowed or allowable from line 22	25a				
b	Enter the **smaller** of line 24 or 25a	25b				
26	**If section 1250 property:** If straight line depreciation was used, enter -0- on line 26g, except for a corporation subject to section 291.					
a	Additional depreciation after 1975 (see instructions)	26a				
b	Applicable percentage multiplied by the **smaller** of line 24 or line 26a (see instructions)	26b				
c	Subtract line 26a from line 24. If residential rental property or line 24 is not more than line 26a, skip lines 26d and 26e	26c				
d	Additional depreciation after 1969 and before 1976	26d				
e	Enter the **smaller** of line 26c or 26d	26e				
f	Section 291 amount (corporations only)	26f				
g	Add lines 26b, 26e, and 26f	26g				
27	**If section 1252 property:** Skip this section if you did not dispose of farmland or if this form is being completed for a partnership (other than an electing large partnership).					
a	Soil, water, and land clearing expenses	27a				
b	Line 27a multiplied by applicable percentage (see instructions)	27b				
c	Enter the **smaller** of line 24 or 27b	27c				
28	**If section 1254 property:**					
a	Intangible drilling and development costs, expenditures for development of mines and other natural deposits, and mining exploration costs (see instructions)	28a				
b	Enter the **smaller** of line 24 or 28a	28b				
29	**If section 1255 property:**					
a	Applicable percentage of payments excluded from income under section 126 (see instructions)	29a				
b	Enter the **smaller** of line 24 or 29a (see instructions)	29b				

Summary of Part III Gains. Complete property columns A through D through line 29b before going to line 30.

30	Total gains for all properties. Add property columns A through D, line 24	30	
31	Add property columns A through D, lines 25b, 26g, 27c, 28b, and 29b. Enter here and on line 13	31	
32	Subtract line 31 from line 30. Enter the portion from casualty or theft on Form 4684, line 33. Enter the portion from other than casualty or theft on Form 4797, line 6	32	

Part IV Recapture Amounts Under Sections 179 and 280F(b)(2) When Business Use Drops to 50% or Less (see instructions)

			(a) Section 179	(b) Section 280F(b)(2)
33	Section 179 expense deduction or depreciation allowable in prior years	33		
34	Recomputed depreciation (see instructions)	34		
35	Recapture amount. Subtract line 34 from line 33. See the instructions for where to report	35		

Form **4562**

Department of the Treasury
Internal Revenue Service (99)

Depreciation and Amortization

(Including Information on Listed Property)

▶ See separate instructions. ▶ Attach to your tax return.

OMB No. 1545-0172

2008

Attachment
Sequence No. **67**

Name(s) shown on return

Business or activity to which this form relates

Identifying number

Part I Election To Expense Certain Property Under Section 179
Note: If you have any listed property, complete Part V before you complete Part I.

1	Maximum amount. See the instructions for a higher limit for certain businesses	1	$250,000
2	Total cost of section 179 property placed in service (see instructions)	2	
3	Threshold cost of section 179 property before reduction in limitation (see instructions)	3	$800,000
4	Reduction in limitation. Subtract line 3 from line 2. If zero or less, enter -0-	4	
5	Dollar limitation for tax year. Subtract line 4 from line 1. If zero or less, enter -0-. If married filing separately, see instructions	5	

(a) Description of property	(b) Cost (business use only)	(c) Elected cost
6		

7	Listed property. Enter the amount from line 29	7	
8	Total elected cost of section 179 property. Add amounts in column (c), lines 6 and 7	8	
9	Tentative deduction. Enter the **smaller** of line 5 or line 8	9	
10	Carryover of disallowed deduction from line 13 of your 2007 Form 4562	10	
11	Business income limitation. Enter the smaller of business income (not less than zero) or line 5 (see instructions)	11	
12	Section 179 expense deduction. Add lines 9 and 10, but do not enter more than line 11	12	
13	Carryover of disallowed deduction to 2009. Add lines 9 and 10, less line 12 ▶	13	

Note: Do not use Part II or Part III below for listed property. Instead, use Part V.

Part II Special Depreciation Allowance and Other Depreciation (Do not include listed property.) (See instructions.)

14	Special depreciation allowance for qualified property (other than listed property) placed in service during the tax year (see instructions)	14	
15	Property subject to section 168(f)(1) election	15	
16	Other depreciation (including ACRS)	16	

Part III MACRS Depreciation (Do not include listed property.) (See instructions.)

Section A

17	MACRS deductions for assets placed in service in tax years beginning before 2008	17	
18	If you are electing to group any assets placed in service during the tax year into one or more general asset accounts, check here ▶ ☐		

Section B—Assets Placed in Service During 2008 Tax Year Using the General Depreciation System

(a) Classification of property	(b) Month and year placed in service	(c) Basis for depreciation (business/investment use only—see instructions)	(d) Recovery period	(e) Convention	(f) Method	(g) Depreciation deduction
19a 3-year property						
b 5-year property						
c 7-year property						
d 10-year property						
e 15-year property						
f 20-year property						
g 25-year property			25 yrs.		S/L	
h Residential rental property			27.5 yrs.	MM	S/L	
			27.5 yrs.	MM	S/L	
i Nonresidential real property			39 yrs.	MM	S/L	
				MM	S/L	

Section C—Assets Placed in Service During 2008 Tax Year Using the Alternative Depreciation System

20a Class life					S/L	
b 12-year			12 yrs.		S/L	
c 40-year			40 yrs.	MM	S/L	

Part IV Summary (See instructions.)

21	Listed property. Enter amount from line 28	21	
22	**Total.** Add amounts from line 12, lines 14 through 17, lines 19 and 20 in column (g), and line 21. Enter here and on the appropriate lines of your return. Partnerships and S corporations—see instr.	22	
23	For assets shown above and placed in service during the current year, enter the portion of the basis attributable to section 263A costs	23	

For Paperwork Reduction Act Notice, see separate instructions.

Cat. No. 12906N

Form **4562** (2008)

Part V   Listed Property (Include automobiles, certain other vehicles, cellular telephones, certain computers, and property used for entertainment, recreation, or amusement.)

     Note: *For any vehicle for which you are using the standard mileage rate or deducting lease expense, complete only 24a, 24b, columns (a) through (c) of Section A, all of Section B, and Section C if applicable.*

Section A—Depreciation and Other Information (Caution: *See the instructions for limits for passenger automobiles.)*

24a Do you have evidence to support the business/investment use claimed? ☐ Yes ☐ No   24b If "Yes," is the evidence written? ☐ Yes ☐ No

(a) Type of property (list vehicles first)	(b) Date placed in service	(c) Business/ investment use percentage	(d) Cost or other basis	(e) Basis for depreciation (business/investment use only)	(f) Recovery period	(g) Method/ Convention	(h) Depreciation deduction	(i) Elected section 179 cost
25 Special depreciation allowance for qualified listed property placed in service during the tax year and used more than 50% in a qualified business use (see instructions)						**25**		
26 Property used more than 50% in a qualified business use:								
		%						
		%						
		%						
27 Property used 50% or less in a qualified business use:								
		%				S/L —		
		%				S/L —		
		%				S/L —		
28 Add amounts in column (h), lines 25 through 27. Enter here and on line 21, page 1 .						**28**		
29 Add amounts in column (i), line 26. Enter here and on line 7, page 1. . . . . **29**								

Section B—Information on Use of Vehicles

Complete this section for vehicles used by a sole proprietor, partner, or other "more than 5% owner," or related person.

If you provided vehicles to your employees, first answer the questions in Section C to see if you meet an exception to completing this section for those vehicles.

	(a) Vehicle 1		(b) Vehicle 2		(c) Vehicle 3		(d) Vehicle 4		(e) Vehicle 5		(f) Vehicle 6	
30 Total business/investment miles driven during the year (**do not** include commuting miles)												
31 Total commuting miles driven during the year												
32 Total other personal (noncommuting) miles driven												
33 Total miles driven during the year. Add lines 30 through 32												
	Yes	No	Yes	No	Yes	No	Yes	No	Yes	No	Yes	No
34 Was the vehicle available for personal use during off-duty hours? . . .												
35 Was the vehicle used primarily by a more than 5% owner or related person?												
36 Is another vehicle available for personal use?												

Section C—Questions for Employers Who Provide Vehicles for Use by Their Employees

Answer these questions to determine if you meet an exception to completing Section B for vehicles used by employees who **are not** more than 5% owners or related persons (see instructions).

		Yes	No
37	Do you maintain a written policy statement that prohibits all personal use of vehicles, including commuting, by your employees?		
38	Do you maintain a written policy statement that prohibits personal use of vehicles, except commuting, by your employees? See the instructions for vehicles used by corporate officers, directors, or 1% or more owners		
39	Do you treat all use of vehicles by employees as personal use?		
40	Do you provide more than five vehicles to your employees, obtain information from your employees about the use of the vehicles, and retain the information received?		
41	Do you meet the requirements concerning qualified automobile demonstration use? (See instructions.)		

     Note: *If your answer to 37, 38, 39, 40, or 41 is "Yes," do not complete Section B for the covered vehicles.*

Part VI   Amortization

(a) Description of costs	(b) Date amortization begins	(c) Amortizable amount	(d) Code section	(e) Amortization period or percentage	(f) Amortization for this year
42 Amortization of costs that begins during your 2008 tax year (see instructions):					
43 Amortization of costs that began before your 2008 tax year **43**					
44 **Total.** Add amounts in column (f). See the instructions for where to report **44**					

Form **6252**	**Installment Sale Income**	OMB No. 1545-0228
Department of the Treasury Internal Revenue Service	▶ Attach to your tax return. ▶ Use a separate form for each sale or other disposition of property on the installment method.	**2008** Attachment Sequence No. **79**

Name(s) shown on return | Identifying number

1 Description of property ▶ ....

2a Date acquired (month, day, year) ▶ ____/____/____ b Date sold (month, day, year) ▶ ____/____/____

3 Was the property sold to a related party (see instructions) after May 14, 1980? If "No," skip line 4 . . . . ☐ Yes ☐ No

4 Was the property you sold to a related party a marketable security? If "Yes," complete Part III. If "No," complete Part III for the year of sale and the 2 years after the year of sale . . . . ☐ Yes ☐ No

Part I   **Gross Profit and Contract Price.** Complete this part for the year of sale only.

5	Selling price including mortgages and other debts. **Do not** include interest whether stated or unstated	5	
6	Mortgages, debts, and other liabilities the buyer assumed or took the property subject to (see instructions)	6	
7	Subtract line 6 from line 5	7	
8	Cost or other basis of property sold	8	
9	Depreciation allowed or allowable	9	
10	Adjusted basis. Subtract line 9 from line 8	10	
11	Commissions and other expenses of sale	11	
12	Income recapture from Form 4797, Part III (see instructions) . .	12	
13	Add lines 10, 11, and 12	13	
14	Subtract line 13 from line 5. If zero or less, **do not** complete the rest of this form (see instructions)	14	
15	If the property described on line 1 above was your main home, enter the amount of your excluded gain (see instructions). Otherwise, enter -0-	15	
16	**Gross profit.** Subtract line 15 from line 14	16	
17	Subtract line 13 from line 6. If zero or less, enter -0-	17	
18	**Contract price.** Add line 7 and line 17	18	

Part II   **Installment Sale Income.** Complete this part for the year of sale **and** any year you receive a payment or have certain debts you must treat as a payment on installment obligations.

19	Gross profit percentage (expressed as a decimal amount). Divide line 16 by line 18. For years after the year of sale, see instructions	19	
20	If this is the year of sale, enter the amount from line 17. Otherwise, enter -0-	20	
21	Payments received during year (see instructions). **Do not** include interest, whether stated or unstated	21	
22	Add lines 20 and 21	22	
23	Payments received in prior years (see instructions). **Do not** include interest, whether stated or unstated	23	
24	**Installment sale income.** Multiply line 22 by line 19	24	
25	Enter the part of line 24 that is ordinary income under the recapture rules (see instructions) .	25	
26	Subtract line 25 from line 24. Enter here and on Schedule D or Form 4797 (see instructions)	26	

Part III   **Related Party Installment Sale Income.** **Do not** complete if you received the final payment this tax year.

27 Name, address, and taxpayer identifying number of related party ....

28 Did the related party resell or dispose of the property ("second disposition") during this tax year? . . . . ☐ Yes ☐ No

29 If the answer to question 28 is "Yes," complete lines 30 through 37 below unless one of the following conditions is met. Check the box that applies.

a ☐ The second disposition was more than 2 years after the first disposition (other than dispositions of marketable securities). If this box is checked, enter the date of disposition (month, day, year) ▶ ____/____/____

b ☐ The first disposition was a sale or exchange of stock to the issuing corporation.

c ☐ The second disposition was an involuntary conversion and the threat of conversion occurred after the first disposition.

d ☐ The second disposition occurred after the death of the original seller or buyer.

e ☐ It can be established to the satisfaction of the Internal Revenue Service that tax avoidance was not a principal purpose for either of the dispositions. If this box is checked, attach an explanation (see instructions).

30	Selling price of property sold by related party (see instructions)	30	
31	Enter contract price from line 18 for year of first sale	31	
32	Enter the **smaller** of line 30 or line 31	32	
33	Total payments received by the end of your 2008 tax year (see instructions)	33	
34	Subtract line 33 from line 32. If zero or less, enter -0-	34	
35	Multiply line 34 by the gross profit percentage on line 19 for year of first sale . . .	35	
36	Enter the part of line 35 that is ordinary income under the recapture rules (see instructions) .	36	
37	Subtract line 36 from line 35. Enter here and on Schedule D or Form 4797 (see instructions)	37	

General Instructions

Section references are to the Internal Revenue Code unless otherwise noted.

Purpose of Form

Generally, use Form 6252 to report income from casual sales during this tax year of real or personal property (other than inventory) if you will receive any payments in a tax year after the year of sale. For years after the year of an installment sale, see *Which Parts To Complete* below.

Do not file Form 6252 for sales that do not result in a gain, even if you will receive a payment in a tax year after the year of sale. Instead, report the entire sale on Form 4797, Sales of Business Property, or the Schedule D for your tax return, whichever applies.

Do not file Form 6252 to report sales during the tax year of stock or securities traded on an established securities market. Instead, treat all payments as received during this tax year.

Do not file Form 6252 if you elect not to report the sale on the installment method. To elect out, report the full amount of the gain on a timely filed return (including extensions) on Form 4797 or the Schedule D for your tax return, whichever applies. If you filed your original return on time without making the election, you can make the election on an amended return filed no later than 6 months after the due date of your tax return, excluding extensions. Write "Filed pursuant to section 301.9100-2" at the top of the amended return.

Which Parts To Complete

Year of Sale

Complete lines 1 through 4, Part I, and Part II. If you sold property to a related party during the year, also complete Part III.

Later Years

Complete lines 1 through 4 and Part II for any year in which you receive a payment from an installment sale.

If you sold a marketable security to a related party after May 14, 1980, and before January 1, 1987, complete Form 6252 for each year of the installment agreement, even if you did not receive a payment. Complete lines 1 through 4. Complete Part II for any year in which you receive a payment from the sale. Complete Part III unless you received the final payment during the tax year.

After December 31, 1986, the installment method is not available for the sale of marketable securities.

If you sold property other than a marketable security to a related party after May 14, 1980, complete Form 6252 for the year of sale and for 2 years after the year of sale, even if you did not receive a payment. Complete lines 1 through 4. Complete Part II for any year during this 2-year period in which you receive a payment from the sale. Complete Part III for the 2 years after the year of sale unless you received the final payment during the tax year.

Special Rules

Interest

If any part of an installment payment you received is for interest or original issue discount, report that income on the appropriate form or schedule. Do not report interest received, carrying charges received, or unstated interest on Form 6252. See Pub. 537, Installment Sales, for details on unstated interest.

Installment Sales to Related Party

A special rule applies to a first disposition (sale or exchange) of property under the installment method to a related party who then makes a second disposition (sale, exchange, gift, or cancellation of installment note) before making all payments on the first disposition. For this purpose, a related party includes your spouse, child, grandchild, parent, brother, sister, or a related corporation, S corporation, partnership, estate, or trust. See section 453(f)(1) for more details.

Under this rule, treat part or all of the amount the related party realized (or the fair market value (FMV) if the disposed property is not sold or exchanged) from the second disposition as if you received it from the first disposition at the time of the second disposition. Figure the gain, if any, on lines 30 through 37. This rule does not apply if any of the conditions listed on line 29 are met.

Sale of Depreciable Property to Related Person

Generally, if you sell depreciable property to a related person (as defined in section 453(g)(3)), you cannot report the sale using the installment method. For this purpose, depreciable property is any property that can be depreciated by a person or entity to whom you transfer it. However, you can use the installment method if you can show to the satisfaction of the IRS that avoidance of federal income taxes was not one of the principal purposes of the sale (for example, no significant tax deferral benefits will result from the sale). If the installment method does not apply, report the sale on Schedule D or Form 4797,

whichever applies. Treat all payments you will receive as if they were received in the year of sale. Use FMV for any payment that is contingent as to amount. If the FMV cannot be readily determined, basis is recovered ratably.

Pledge Rule

For certain dispositions under the installment method, if an installment obligation is pledged as security on a debt, the net proceeds of the secured debt are treated as payment on the installment obligation. However, the amount treated as payment cannot be more than the excess of the total installment contract price over any payments received under the contract before the secured debt was obtained.

An installment obligation is pledged as security on a debt to the extent that payment of principal and interest on the debt is directly secured by an interest in the installment obligation. For sales after December 16, 1999, payment on a debt is treated as directly secured by an interest in an installment obligation to the extent an arrangement allows you to satisfy all or part of the debt with the installment obligation.

The pledge rule applies to any installment sale after 1988 with a sales price of over $150,000 except:

- Personal use property disposed of by an individual,
- Farm property, and
- Timeshares and residential lots.

However, the pledge rule does not apply to pledges made after December 17, 1987, if the debt is incurred to refinance the principal amount of a debt that was outstanding on December 17, 1987, and was secured by nondealer real property installment obligations on that date and at all times after that date until the refinancing. This exception does not apply to the extent that the principal amount of the debt resulting from the refinancing exceeds the principal amount of the refinanced debt immediately before the refinancing. Also, the pledge rule does not affect refinancing due to the calling of a debt by the creditor if the debt is then refinanced by a person other than this creditor or someone related to the creditor.

Interest on Deferred Tax

Generally, you must pay interest on the deferred tax related to any obligation that arises during a tax year from the disposition of property under the installment method if:

- The property had a sales price over $150,000, and

- The aggregate balance of all nondealer installment obligations arising during, and outstanding at the close of, the tax year is more than $5 million.

You must pay interest in subsequent years if installment obligations that originally required interest to be paid are still outstanding at the close of a tax year.

The interest rules do not apply to dispositions of:

- Farm property,
- Personal use property by an individual,
- Real property before 1988, or
- Personal property before 1989.

See IRC 453(f) for more information on the sale of timeshares and residential lots under the installment method.

How to report the interest. The interest is not figured on Form 6252. See Pub. 537, Installment Sales, for details on how to report the interest.

Additional Information

See Pub. 537 for additional information, including details about reductions in selling price, the single sale of several assets, like-kind exchanges, dispositions of installment obligations, and repossessions.

Specific Instructions

Part I—Gross Profit and Contract Price

Line 5

Enter the total of any money, face amount of the installment obligation, and the FMV of other property that you received or will receive in exchange for the property sold. Include on line 5 any existing mortgage or other debt the buyer assumed or took the property subject to. Do not include stated interest, unstated interest, any amount recomputed or recharacterized as interest, or original issue discount.

If there is no stated maximum selling price, such as in a contingent payment sale, attach a schedule showing the computation of gain. Enter the taxable part of the payment on line 24 and also on line 35 if Part III applies. See Temporary Regulations section 15A.453-1.

Line 6

Enter only mortgages or other debts the buyer assumed from the seller or took the property subject to. Do not include new mortgages the buyer gets from a bank, the seller, or other sources.

Line 8

Enter the original cost and other expenses you incurred in buying the property. Add the cost of improvements, etc., and subtract any diesel-powered highway vehicle, enhanced oil recovery,

disabled access, new markets, or employer-provided child care credit or casualty losses previously allowed. For details, see Pub. 551, Basis of Assets.

Line 9

Enter all depreciation or amortization you deducted or were allowed to deduct from the date of purchase until the date of sale. Add any section 179 expense deduction; the commercial revitalization deduction; the basis reduction to investment credit property; the deduction for qualified clean-fuel vehicle property or refueling property; deductions claimed under section 190, 193, or 1253(d)(2) or (3) (as in effect before the enactment of P.L. 103-66); and the basis reduction for the qualified electric vehicle credit. Subtract any recapture of basis reduction to investment credit property; any section 179 or 280F recapture amount included in gross income in a prior tax year; any qualified clean-fuel vehicle property or refueling property deduction you were required to recapture because the property ceased to be eligible for the deduction; any recapture of the employer-provided child care facilities and services credit; and any basis increase for qualified electric vehicle recapture.

Line 11

Enter sales commissions, advertising expenses, attorney and legal fees, etc., incurred to sell the property.

Line 12

Any ordinary income recapture under section 1245 or 1250 (including sections 179 and 291) is fully taxable in the year of sale even if no payments were received. To figure the recapture amount, complete Form 4797, Part III. The ordinary income recapture is the amount on line 31 of Form 4797. Enter it on line 12 of Form 6252 and also on line 13 of Form 4797. Do not enter any gain for this property on line 32 of Form 4797. If you used Form 4797 only to figure the recapture amount on line 12 of Form 6252, enter "N/A" on line 32 of Form 4797. Partnerships and S corporations and their partners and shareholders, see the Instructions for Form 4797.

Line 14

Do not file Form 6252 if line 14 is zero or less. Instead, report the entire sale on Form 4797 or the Schedule D for your tax return.

Line 15

If the property described on line 1 was your main home, you may be able to exclude part or all of your gain. See Pub. 523, Selling Your Home, for details.

Part II—Installment Sale Income

Line 19

Enter the gross profit percentage (expressed as a decimal amount) determined for the year of sale even if you did not file Form 6252 for that year.

Line 21

Enter all money and the FMV of any property you received in 2008. Include as payments any amount withheld to pay off a mortgage or other debt or to pay broker and legal fees. Generally, do not include as a payment the buyer's note, a mortgage, or other debt assumed by the buyer. However, a note or other debt that is payable on demand or readily tradable in an established securities market is considered a payment. For sales occurring before October 22, 2004, a note or other debt is considered a payment only if it was issued by a corporation or governmental entity. If you did not receive any payments in 2008, enter zero. If in prior years an amount was entered on the equivalent of line 32 of the 2008 form, do not include it on this line. Instead, enter it on line 23. See *Pledge Rule* on page 2 for details about proceeds of debt secured by installment obligations that must be treated as payments on installment obligations.

Line 23

Enter all money and the FMV of property you received before 2008 from the sale. Include allocable installment income and any other deemed payments from prior years.

Deemed payments include amounts deemed received because of:

- A second disposition by a related party, or
- The pledge rule of section 453A(d).

Line 25

Enter here and on Form 4797, line 15, any ordinary income recapture on section 1252, 1254, or 1255 property for the year of sale or all remaining recapture from a prior year sale. Do not enter ordinary income from a section 179 expense deduction. If this is the year of sale, complete Form 4797, Part III. The amount from line 27c, 28b, or 29b of Form 4797 is the ordinary income recapture. Do not enter any gain for this property on line 31 or 32 of Form 4797. If you used Form 4797 only to figure the recapture on line 25 or 36 of Form 6252, enter "N/A" on lines 31 and 32 of Form 4797.

Also report on this line any ordinary income recapture remaining from prior years on section 1245 or 1250 property sold before June 7, 1984.

Do not enter on line 25 more than the amount shown on line 24. Any excess must be reported in future years on Form 6252 up to the taxable part of the installment sale until all of the recapture has been reported.

Line 26

For trade or business property held more than 1 year, enter this amount on Form 4797, line 4. If the property was held 1 year or less or you have an ordinary gain from the sale of a noncapital asset (even if the holding period is more than 1 year), enter this amount on Form 4797, line 10, and write "From Form 6252." If the property was section 1250 property (generally, real property that you depreciated) held more than 1 year, figure the total amount of unrecaptured section 1250 gain included on line 26 using the *Unrecaptured Section 1250 Gain Worksheet* in the Instructions for Schedule D (Form 1040).

For capital assets, enter this amount on Schedule D as a short- or long-term gain on the lines identified as from Form 6252.

Part III—Related Party Installment Sale Income

Line 29

If one of the conditions is met, check the appropriate box and skip lines 30 through 37. If you checked box 29e, attach an explanation. Generally, the nontax avoidance exception will apply to the second disposition if:

● The disposition was involuntary (for example, a creditor of the related party foreclosed on the property or the related party declared bankruptcy), or

● The disposition was an installment sale under which the terms of payment were substantially equal to or longer than those for the first sale. However, the resale terms must not permit significant deferral of recognition of gain from the first sale (for example, amounts from the resale are being collected sooner).

Line 30

If the related party sold all or part of the property from the original sale in 2008, enter the amount realized from the part resold. If part was sold in an earlier year and part was sold this year, enter the cumulative amount realized from the resale.

Amount realized. The amount realized from a sale or exchange is the total of all money received plus the FMV of all property or services received. The amount realized also includes any liabilities that were assumed by the buyer and any liabilities to which the property transferred is subject, such as real estate taxes or a mortgage. For details, see Pub. 544.

Line 33

If you completed Part II, enter the sum of lines 22 and 23. Otherwise, enter all money and the FMV of property you received before 2008 from the sale. Include allocable installment income and any other deemed payments from prior years. Do not include interest, whether stated or unstated.

Line 36

See the instructions for line 25. Do not enter on line 36 more than the amount shown on line 35. Any excess must be reported in future years on Form 6252 up to the taxable part of the installment sale until all of the recapture has been reported.

Line 37

See the instructions for line 26.

Paperwork Reduction Act Notice. We ask for the information on this form to carry out the Internal Revenue laws of the United States. You are required to give us the information. We need it to ensure that you are complying with these laws and to allow us to figure and collect the right amount of tax.

You are not required to provide the information requested on a form that is subject to the Paperwork Reduction Act unless the form displays a valid OMB control number. Books or records relating to a form or its instructions must be retained as long as their contents may become material in the administration of any Internal Revenue law. Generally, tax returns and return information are confidential, as required by section 6103.

The time needed to complete and file this form will vary depending on individual circumstances. The estimated burden for individual taxpayers filing this form is approved under OMB control number 1545-0074 and is included in the estimates shown in the instructions for their individual income tax return. The estimated burden for all other taxpayers who file this form is shown below.

Recordkeeping . . . . 1 hr., 18 min.

**Learning about the law
or the form** . . . . 24 min.

Preparing the form . . . . . . 1 hr.

**Copying, assembling, and
sending the form
to the IRS** . . . . 20 min.

If you have comments concerning the accuracy of these time estimates or suggestions for making this form simpler, we would be happy to hear from you. See the instructions for the tax return with which this form is filed.

Form **8824**

Department of the Treasury
Internal Revenue Service

Like-Kind Exchanges

(and section 1043 conflict-of-interest sales)

▶ Attach to your tax return.

OMB No. 1545-1190

2007

Attachment
Sequence No. **109**

Name(s) shown on tax return

Identifying number

Part I	Information on the Like-Kind Exchange

Note: *If the property described on line 1 or line 2 is real or personal property located outside the United States, indicate the country.*

1 Description of like-kind property given up ▶

2 Description of like-kind property received ▶

3 Date like-kind property given up was originally acquired (month, day, year) . . . . . .   **3** ___ / ___ / ___

4 Date you actually transferred your property to other party (month, day, year) . . . . . .   **4** ___ / ___ / ___

5 Date like-kind property you received was identified by written notice to another party (month, day, year). See instructions for 45-day written notice requirement . . . .   **5** ___ / ___ / ___

6 Date you actually received the like-kind property from other party (month, day, year). See instructions   **6** ___ / ___ / ___

7 Was the exchange of the property given up or received made with a related party, either directly or indirectly (such as through an intermediary)? See instructions. If "Yes," complete Part II. If "No," go to Part III . . . ☐ Yes ☐ No

Part II	Related Party Exchange Information

8

Name of related party	Relationship to you	Related party's identifying number

Address (no., street, and apt., room, or suite no., city or town, state, and ZIP code)

9 During this tax year (and before the date that is 2 years after the last transfer of property that was part of the exchange), did the related party directly or indirectly (such as through an intermediary) sell or dispose of any part of the like-kind property received from you in the exchange? . . . . ☐ Yes ☐ No

10 During this tax year (and before the date that is 2 years after the last transfer of property that was part of the exchange), did you sell or dispose of any part of the like-kind property you received? . . . . ☐ Yes ☐ No

*If both lines 9 and 10 are "No" and this is the year of the exchange, go to Part III. If both lines 9 and 10 are "No" and this is not the year of the exchange, stop here. If either line 9 or line 10 is "Yes," complete Part III and report on this year's tax return the deferred gain or (loss) from line 24 **unless** one of the exceptions on line 11 applies.*

11 If one of the exceptions below applies to the disposition, check the applicable box:

a ☐ The disposition was after the death of either of the related parties.

b ☐ The disposition was an involuntary conversion, and the threat of conversion occurred after the exchange.

c ☐ You can establish to the satisfaction of the IRS that neither the exchange nor the disposition had tax avoidance as its principal purpose. If this box is checked, attach an explanation (see instructions).

For Paperwork Reduction Act Notice, see page 5.   Cat. No. 12311A   Form **8824** (2007)

Name(s) shown on tax return. Do not enter name and social security number if shown on other side.	Your social security number

Part III　Realized Gain or (Loss), Recognized Gain, and Basis of Like-Kind Property Received

Caution: *If you transferred* **and** *received* **(a)** *more than one group of like-kind properties or* **(b)** *cash or other (not like-kind) property, see* **Reporting of multi-asset exchanges** *in the instructions.*

Note: *Complete lines 12 through 14* **only** *if you gave up property that was not like-kind. Otherwise, go to line 15.*

12	Fair market value (FMV) of other property given up	**12**	
13	Adjusted basis of other property given up	**13**	
14	Gain or (loss) recognized on other property given up. Subtract line 13 from line 12. Report the gain or (loss) in the same manner as if the exchange had been a sale . . . . **Caution:** *If the property given up was used previously or partly as a home, see* **Property used as home** *in the instructions.*	**14**	
15	Cash received, FMV of other property received, plus net liabilities assumed by other party, reduced (but not below zero) by any exchange expenses you incurred (see instructions)	**15**	
16	FMV of like-kind property you received	**16**	
17	Add lines 15 and 16	**17**	
18	Adjusted basis of like-kind property you gave up, net amounts paid to other party, plus any exchange expenses **not** used on line 15 (see instructions)	**18**	
19	**Realized gain or (loss).** Subtract line 18 from line 17	**19**	
20	Enter the smaller of line 15 or line 19, but not less than zero	**20**	
21	Ordinary income under recapture rules. Enter here and on Form 4797, line 16 (see instructions) .	**21**	
22	Subtract line 21 from line 20. If zero or less, enter -0-. If more than zero, enter here and on Schedule D or Form 4797, unless the installment method applies (see instructions) . . .	**22**	
23	**Recognized gain.** Add lines 21 and 22	**23**	
24	Deferred gain or (loss). Subtract line 23 from line 19. If a related party exchange, see instructions	**24**	
25	**Basis of like-kind property received.** Subtract line 15 from the sum of lines 18 and 23 . .	**25**	

Part IV　Deferral of Gain From Section 1043 Conflict-of-Interest Sales

Note: *This part is to be used* **only** *by officers or employees of the executive branch of the Federal Government or judicial officers of the Federal Government for reporting nonrecognition of gain under section 1043 on the sale of property to comply with the conflict-of-interest requirements. This part can be used* **only** *if the cost of the replacement property is more than the basis of the divested property.*

26	Enter the number from the upper right corner of your certificate of divestiture. (**Do not** attach a copy of your certificate. Keep the certificate with your records.). . . . . ▶	_____ - _____
27	Description of divested property ▶	
28	Description of replacement property ▶	

29	Date divested property was sold (month, day, year)	**29**	/ /
30	Sales price of divested property (see instructions)	**30**	
31	Basis of divested property	**31**	
32	**Realized gain.** Subtract line 31 from line 30	**32**	
33	Cost of replacement property purchased within 60 days after date of sale	**33**	
34	Subtract line 33 from line 30. If zero or less, enter -0-	**34**	
35	Ordinary income under recapture rules. Enter here and on Form 4797, line 10 (see instructions)	**35**	
36	Subtract line 35 from line 34. If zero or less, enter -0-. If more than zero, enter here and on Schedule D or Form 4797 (see instructions)	**36**	
37	**Deferred gain.** Subtract the sum of lines 35 and 36 from line 32	**37**	
38	**Basis of replacement property.** Subtract line 37 from line 33	**38**	

General Instructions

Section references are to the Internal Revenue Code unless otherwise noted.

What's New

Judicial officers. If you are a judicial officer of the Federal Government and you sell property at a gain after December 20, 2006, according to a certificate of divestiture issued by the Judicial Conference of the United States (or its designee) and purchase replacement property (permitted property) within 60 days after the sale, you can elect to defer part or all of the realized gain. This election also applies to sales by certain persons related to the judicial officer and to sales by trustees of certain trusts in which the judicial officer or related person has a beneficial interest. Use Part IV to report these sales.

Purpose of Form

Use Parts I, II, and III of Form 8824 to report each exchange of business or investment property for property of a like kind. Certain members of the executive branch of the Federal Government and judicial officers of the Federal Government use Part IV to elect to defer gain on conflict-of-interest sales. Judicial officers of the Federal Government are the following:

  1. Chief Justice of the United States.

  2. Associate Justices of the Supreme Court.

  3. Judges of the:

    a. United States courts of appeals,

    b. United States district courts, including the district courts in Guam, the Northern Mariana Islands, and the Virgin Islands,

    c. Court of Appeals for the Federal Circuit,

    d. Court of International Trade,

    e. Tax Court,

    f. Court of Federal Claims,

    g. Court of Appeals for Veterans Claims,

    h. United States Court of Appeals for the Armed Forces, and

    i. Any court created by Act of Congress, the judges of which are entitled to hold office during good behavior.

Multiple exchanges. If you made more than one like-kind exchange, you can file only a summary Form 8824 and attach your own statement showing all the information requested on Form 8824 for each exchange. Include your name and identifying number at the top of each page of the statement. On the summary Form 8824, enter only your name and identifying number, "Summary" on line 1, the total recognized gain from all exchanges on line 23, and the total basis of all like-kind property received on line 25.

When To File

If during the current tax year you transferred property to another party in a like-kind exchange, you must file Form 8824 with your tax return for that year. Also file Form 8824 for the 2 years following the year of a related party exchange (see the instructions for line 7 on page 4).

Like-Kind Exchanges

Generally, if you exchange business or investment property solely for business or investment property of a like kind, section 1031 provides that no gain or loss is recognized. If, as part of the exchange, you also receive other (not like-kind) property or money, gain is recognized to the extent of the other property and money received, but a loss is not recognized.

Section 1031 does not apply to exchanges of inventory, stocks, bonds, notes, other securities or evidence of indebtedness, or certain other assets. See section 1031(a)(2). In addition, section 1031 does not apply to certain exchanges involving tax-exempt use property subject to a lease. See section 470(e)(4).

Like-kind property. Properties are of like kind if they are of the same nature or character, even if they differ in grade or quality. Personal properties of a like class are like-kind properties. However, livestock of different sexes are not like-kind properties. Also, personal property used predominantly in the United States and personal property used predominantly outside the United States are not like-kind properties. See Pub. 544, Sales and Other Dispositions of Assets, for more details.

Real properties generally are of like kind, regardless of whether they are improved or unimproved. However, real property in the United States and real property outside the United States are not like-kind properties.

Deferred exchanges. A deferred exchange occurs when the property received in the exchange is received after the transfer of the property given up. For a deferred exchange to qualify as like-kind, you must comply with the 45-day written notice and receipt requirements explained in the instructions for line 5 and line 6 on page 4.

Multi-asset exchanges. A multi-asset exchange involves the transfer and receipt of more than one group of like-kind properties. For example, an exchange of land, vehicles, and cash for land and vehicles is a multi-asset exchange. An exchange of land, vehicles, and cash for land only is not a multi-asset exchange. The transfer or receipt of multiple properties within one like-kind group is also a multi-asset exchange. Special rules apply when figuring the amount of gain recognized and your basis in properties received in a multi-asset exchange. For details, see Regulations section 1.1031(j)-1.

  Reporting of multi-asset exchanges. If you transferred and received (a) more than one group of like-kind properties or (b) cash or other (not like-kind) property, do not complete lines 12 through 18 of Form 8824. Instead, attach your own statement showing how you figured the realized and recognized gain, and enter the correct amount on lines 19 through 25. Report any recognized gains on Schedule D; Form 4797, Sales of Business Property; or Form 6252, Installment Sale Income, whichever applies.

Exchanges using a qualified exchange accommodation arrangement (QEAA). If property is transferred to an exchange accommodation titleholder (EAT) and held in a QEAA, the EAT may be treated as the beneficial owner of the property, the property transferred from the EAT to you may be treated as property you received in an exchange, and the property you transferred to the EAT may be treated as property you gave up in an exchange. This may be true even if the property you are to receive is transferred to the EAT before you transfer the property you are giving up. However, the property transferred to you cannot be treated as property received in an exchange if you previously owned it within 180 days of its transfer to the EAT. For details, see Rev. Proc. 2000-37 as modified by Rev. Proc. 2004-51. Rev. Proc. 2000-37 is on page 308 of Internal Revenue Bulletin 2000-40 at *www.irs.gov/pub/irs-irbs/irb00-40.pdf.* Rev. Proc. 2004-51 is on page 294 of Internal Revenue Bulletin 2004-33 at *www.irs.gov/irb/2004-33_IRB/ar13.html.*

Property used as home. If the property given up was owned and used as your home during the 5-year period ending on the date of the exchange, you may be able to exclude part or all of any gain figured on Form 8824. For details on the exclusion (including how to figure the amount of the exclusion), see Pub. 523, Selling Your Home. Fill out Form 8824 according to its instructions, with these exceptions:

  1. Subtract line 18 from line 17. Subtract the amount of the exclusion from the result. Enter that result on line 19. On the dotted line next to line 19, enter "Section 121 exclusion" and the amount of the exclusion.

  2. On line 20, enter the smaller of:

    a. Line 15 minus the exclusion, or

    b. Line 19.

    Do not enter less than zero.

  3. Subtract line 15 from the sum of lines 18 and 23. Add the amount of your exclusion to the result. Enter that sum on line 25.

  Property used partly as home. If the property given up was used partly as a home, you will need to use two separate Forms 8824 as worksheets—one for the part of the property used as a home and one for the part used for business or investment. Fill out only lines 15 through 25 of each worksheet Form 8824. On the worksheet Form 8824 for the part of the property used as a home, follow steps (1) through (3) above, except that instead of following step (2), enter the amount from line 19 on line 20. On the worksheet Form 8824 for the part of the property used for business or investment, follow steps (1) through (3) above only if you can exclude at least part of any gain from the exchange of that part of the property; otherwise, complete the form according to its instructions. Enter the combined amounts from lines 15 through 25 of both worksheet Forms 8824 on the Form 8824 you file. Do not file either worksheet Form 8824.

More information. For details, see Rev. Proc. 2005-14 on page 528 of Internal Revenue Bulletin 2005-7 at *www.irs.gov/irb/2005-07_IRB/ar10.html.*

Additional information. For more information on like-kind exchanges, see section 1031 and its regulations and Pub. 544.

Specific Instructions

Lines 1 and 2. For real property, enter the address and type of property. For personal property, enter a short description. For property located outside the United States, include the country.

Line 5. Enter on line 5 the date of the written notice that identifies the like-kind property you received in a deferred exchange. To comply with the **45-day written notice requirement,** the following conditions must be met.

1. The like-kind property you receive in a deferred exchange must be designated in writing as replacement property either in a document you signed or in a written agreement signed by all parties to the exchange.

2. The document or agreement must describe the replacement property in a clear and recognizable manner. Real property should be described using a legal description, street address, or distinguishable name (for example, "Mayfair Apartment Building").

3. No later than 45 days after the date you transferred the property you gave up:

a. You must send, fax, or hand deliver the document you signed to the person required to transfer the replacement property to you (including a disqualified person) or to another person involved in the exchange (other than a disqualified person), or

b. All parties to the exchange must sign the written agreement designating the replacement property.

Generally, a disqualified person is either your agent at the time of the transaction or a person related to you. For more details, see Regulations section 1.1031(k)-1(k).

Note. If you received the replacement property before the end of the 45-day period, you automatically are treated as having met the 45-day written notice requirement. In this case, enter on line 5 the date you received the replacement property.

Line 6. Enter on line 6 the date you received the like-kind property from the other party.

The property must be received by the earlier of the following dates.

● The 180th day after the date you transferred the property given up in the exchange.

● The due date (including extensions) of your tax return for the year in which you transferred the property given up.

Line 7. Special rules apply to like-kind exchanges made with related parties, either directly or indirectly. A **related party** includes your spouse, child, grandchild, parent, grandparent, brother, sister, or a related corporation, S corporation, partnership, trust, or estate. See section 1031(f).

An exchange made **indirectly** with a related party includes:

● An exchange made with a related party through an intermediary (such as a qualified intermediary or an exchange accommodation titleholder, as defined in Pub. 544), or

● An exchange made by a disregarded entity (such as a single member limited liability company) if you or a related party owned that entity.

If the related party (either directly or indirectly) or you dispose of the property received in an exchange before the date that is 2 years after the last transfer of property from the exchange, the deferred gain or (loss) from line 24 must be reported on your return for the year of disposition (unless an exception on line 11 applies).

If you are filing this form for 1 of the 2 years following the year of the exchange, complete Parts I and II. If both lines 9 and 10 are "No," **stop.**

If either line 9 or line 10 is "Yes," and an exception on line 11 applies, check the applicable box on line 11, attach any required explanation, and **stop.** If no line 11 exceptions apply, complete Part III. Report the deferred gain or (loss) from line 24 on this year's tax return as if the exchange had been a sale.

An exchange structured to avoid the related party rules is not a like-kind exchange. Do not report it on Form 8824. Instead, you should report the disposition of the property given up as if the exchange had been a sale. See section 1031(f)(4). Such an exchange includes the transfer of property you gave up to a qualified intermediary in exchange for property you received that was formerly owned by a related party if the related party received cash or other (not like-kind) property for the property you received, and you used the qualified intermediary to avoid the application of the related party rules. See Rev. Rul. 2002-83 for more details. You can find Rev. Rul. 2002-83 on page 927 of Internal Revenue Bulletin 2002-49 at *www.irs.gov/pub/irs-irbs/irb02-49.pdf.*

Line 11c. If you believe that you can establish to the satisfaction of the IRS that tax avoidance was not a principal purpose of both the exchange and the disposition, attach an explanation. Generally, tax avoidance will not be seen as a principal purpose in the case of:

● A disposition of property in a nonrecognition transaction.

● An exchange in which the related parties derive no tax advantage from the shifting of basis between the exchanged properties, or

● An exchange of undivided interests in different properties that results in each related party holding either the entire interest in a single property or a larger undivided interest in any of the properties.

Lines 12, 13, and 14. If you gave up other property in addition to the like-kind property, enter the fair market value (FMV) and the adjusted basis of the other property on lines 12 and 13, respectively. The gain or (loss) from this property is figured on line 14 and must be reported on your return. Report gain or (loss) as if the exchange were a sale.

Line 15. Include on line 15 the sum of:

● Any cash paid to you by the other party,

● The FMV of other (not like-kind) property you received, if any, and

● Net liabilities assumed by the other party—the excess, if any, of liabilities (including mortgages) assumed by the other party over the total of (a) any liabilities you assumed, (b) cash you paid to the other party, and (c) the FMV of the other (not like-kind) property you gave up.

Reduce the sum of the above amounts (but not below zero) by any exchange expenses you incurred. See the example on this page.

The following rules apply in determining the amount of liability treated as assumed.

● A recourse liability (or portion thereof) is treated as assumed by the party receiving the property if that party has agreed to and is expected to satisfy the liability (or portion thereof). It does not matter whether the party transferring the property has been relieved of the liability.

● A nonrecourse liability generally is treated as assumed by the party receiving the property subject to the liability. However, if an owner of other assets subject to the same liability agrees with the party receiving the property to, and is expected to, satisfy part or all of the liability, the amount treated as assumed is reduced by the smaller of (a) the amount of the liability that the owner of the other assets has agreed to and is expected to satisfy or (b) the FMV of those other assets.

Line 18. Include on line 18 the sum of:

● The adjusted basis of the like-kind property you gave up,

● Exchange expenses, if any (except for expenses used to reduce the amount reported on line 15), and

● Net amount paid to the other party—the **excess,** if any, of the total of (a) any liabilities you assumed, (b) cash you paid to the other party, and (c) the FMV of the other (not like-kind) property you gave up **over** any liabilities assumed by the other party.

See Regulations section 1.1031(d)-2 and the following example for figuring amounts to enter on lines 15 and 18.

Example. A owns an apartment house with an FMV of $220,000, an adjusted basis of $100,000, and subject to a mortgage of $80,000. B owns an apartment house with an FMV of $250,000, an adjusted basis of $175,000, and subject to a mortgage of $150,000.

A transfers his apartment house to B and receives in exchange B's apartment house plus $40,000 cash. A assumes the mortgage on the apartment house received from B, and B assumes the mortgage on the apartment house received from A.

A enters on line 15 only the $40,000 cash received from B. The $80,000 of liabilities assumed by B is not included because it does not exceed the $150,000 of liabilities A assumed. A enters $170,000 on line 18—the $100,000 adjusted basis, plus the $70,000 excess of the liabilities A assumed over the liabilities assumed by B ($150,000 - $80,000).

B enters $30,000 on line 15—the excess of the $150,000 of liabilities assumed by A over the total ($120,000) of the $80,000 of liabilities B assumed and the $40,000 cash B paid. B enters on line 18 only the adjusted basis of $175,000 because the total of the $80,000 of liabilities B assumed and the $40,000 cash B paid does not exceed the $150,000 of liabilities assumed by A.

Line 21. If you disposed of section 1245, 1250, 1252, 1254, or 1255 property (see the instructions for Part III of Form 4797), you may be required to recapture as ordinary income part or all of the realized gain (line 19). Figure the amount to enter on line 21 as follows:

Section 1245 property. Enter the smaller of:

1. The total adjustments for deductions (whether for the same or other property) allowed or allowable to you or any other person for depreciation or amortization (up to the amount of gain shown on line 19), or

2. The gain shown on line 20, if any, plus the FMV of non-section 1245 like-kind property received.

Section 1250 property. Enter the smaller of:

1. The gain you would have had to report as ordinary income because of additional depreciation if you had sold the property (see the Form 4797 instructions for line 26), or

2. The larger of:

a. The gain shown on line 20, if any, or

b. The excess, if any, of the gain in item (1) above over the FMV of the section 1250 property received.

Section 1252, 1254, and 1255 property. The rules for these types of property are similar to those for section 1245 property. See Regulations section 1.1252-2(d) and Temporary Regulations section 16A.1255-2(c) for details. If the installment method applies to this exchange:

1. See section 453(f)(6) to determine the installment sale income taxable for this year and report it on Form 6252.

2. Enter on Form 6252, line 25 or 36, the section 1252, 1254, or 1255 recapture amount you figured on Form 8824, line 21. Do not enter more than the amount shown on Form 6252, line 24 or 35.

3. Also enter this amount on Form 4797, line 15.

4. If all the ordinary income is not recaptured this year, report in future years on Form 6252 the ordinary income up to the taxable installment sale income, until it is all reported.

Line 22. Report a gain from the exchange of property used in a trade or business (and other noncapital assets) on Form 4797, line 5 or line 16. Report a gain from the exchange of capital assets according to the Schedule D instructions for your return. Be sure to use the date of the exchange as the date for reporting the gain. If the installment method applies to this exchange, see section 453(f)(6) to determine the installment sale income taxable for this year and report it on Form 6252.

Line 24. If line 19 is a loss, enter it on line 24. Otherwise, subtract the amount on line 23 from the amount on line 19 and enter the result. For exchanges with related parties, see the instructions for line 7 on page 4.

Line 25. The amount on line 25 is your basis in the like-kind property you received in the exchange. Your basis in other property received in the exchange, if any, is its FMV.

Section 1043 Conflict-of-Interest Sales (Part IV)

If you sell property at a gain according to a certificate of divestiture issued by the Office of Government Ethics (OGE) or the Judicial Conference of the United States (or its designee) and purchase replacement property (permitted property), you can elect to defer part or all of the realized gain. You must recognize gain on the sale only to the extent that the amount realized on the sale is more than the cost of replacement property purchased within 60 days after the sale. (You also must recognize any ordinary income recapture.) Permitted property is any obligation of the United States or any diversified investment fund approved by the OGE.

 If the property you sold was stock you acquired by exercising a statutory stock option, you may be treated as meeting the holding periods that apply to such stock, regardless of how long you actually held the stock. This may benefit you if you do not defer your entire gain, because it may allow you to treat the gain as a capital gain instead of ordinary income. For details, see section 421(d) or Pub. 525.

Complete Part IV of Form 8824 only if the cost of the replacement property is more than the basis of the divested property and you elect to defer the gain. Otherwise, report the sale on Schedule D or Form 4797, whichever applies.

Your basis in the replacement property is reduced by the amount of the deferred gain. If you made more than one purchase of replacement property, reduce your basis in the replacement property in the order you acquired it.

Line 30. Enter the amount you received from the sale of the divested property, minus any selling expenses.

Line 35. Follow these steps to determine the amount to enter.

1. Use Part III of Form 4797 as a worksheet to figure ordinary income under the recapture rules.

2. Enter on Form 8824, line 35, the amount from Form 4797, line 31. Do not attach the Form 4797 used as a worksheet to your return.

3. Report the amount from line 35 on Form 4797, line 10, column (g). In column (a), write "From Form 8824, line 35." Do not complete columns (b) through (f).

Line 36. If you sold a capital asset, enter any capital gain from line 36 on Schedule D. If you sold property used in a trade or business (or any other asset for which the gain is treated as ordinary income), report the gain on Form 4797, line 2 or line 10, column (g). In column (a), write "From Form 8824, line 36." Do not complete columns (b) through (f).

Paperwork Reduction Act Notice. We ask for the information on this form to carry out the Internal Revenue laws of the United States. You are required to give us the information. We need it to ensure that you are complying with these laws and to allow us to figure and collect the right amount of tax.

You are not required to provide the information requested on a form that is subject to the Paperwork Reduction Act unless the form displays a valid OMB control number. Books or records relating to a form or its instructions must be retained as long as their contents may become material in the administration of any Internal Revenue law. Generally, tax returns and return information are confidential, as required by section 6103.

The time needed to complete and file this form will vary depending on individual circumstances. The estimated burden for individual taxpayers filing this form is approved under OMB control number 1545-0074 and is included in the estimates shown in the instructions for their individual income tax return. The estimated burden for all other taxpayers who file this form is shown below.

Recordkeeping . . . . 10 hr., 45 min.

Learning about the law or the form . . . . 2 hr., 17 min.

Preparing the form . . . 2 hr., 33 min.

Copying, assembling, and sending the form to the IRS . 10 min.

If you have comments concerning the accuracy of these time estimates or suggestions for making this form simpler, we would be happy to hear from you. See the instructions for the tax return with which this form is filed.

SCHEDULE D
(Form 1040)

Department of the Treasury
Internal Revenue Service   (99)

Capital Gains and Losses

► Attach to Form 1040 or Form 1040NR.   ► See Instructions for Schedule D (Form 1040).

► Use Schedule D-1 to list additional transactions for lines 1 and 8.

OMB No. 1545-0074

2008

Attachment
Sequence No. 12

Name(s) shown on return

Your social security number

Part I   Short-Term Capital Gains and Losses—Assets Held One Year or Less

(a) Description of property (Example: 100 sh. XYZ Co.)	(b) Date acquired (Mo., day, yr.)	(c) Date sold (Mo., day, yr.)	(d) Sales price (see page D-7 of the instructions)	(e) Cost or other basis (see page D-7 of the instructions)	(f) Gain or (loss) Subtract (e) from (d)
1					

2   Enter your short-term totals, if any, from Schedule D-1, line 2 . . . . **2**

3   **Total short-term sales price amounts.** Add lines 1 and 2 in column (d) **3**

4   Short-term gain from Form 6252 and short-term gain or (loss) from Forms 4684, 6781, and 8824 . **4**

5   Net short-term gain or (loss) from partnerships, S corporations, estates, and trusts from Schedule(s) K-1 . . . . **5**

6   Short-term capital loss carryover. Enter the amount, if any, from line 8 of your **Capital Loss Carryover Worksheet** on page D-7 of the instructions . . . . **6** ( )

7   **Net short-term capital gain or (loss).** Combine lines 1 through 6 in column (f) **7**

Part II   Long-Term Capital Gains and Losses—Assets Held More Than One Year

(a) Description of property (Example: 100 sh. XYZ Co.)	(b) Date acquired (Mo., day, yr.)	(c) Date sold (Mo., day, yr.)	(d) Sales price (see page D-7 of the instructions)	(e) Cost or other basis (see page D-7 of the instructions)	(f) Gain or (loss) Subtract (e) from (d)
8					

9   Enter your long-term totals, if any, from Schedule D-1, line 9 . . . . **9**

10   **Total long-term sales price amounts.** Add lines 8 and 9 in column (d) **10**

11   Gain from Form 4797, Part I; long-term gain from Forms 2439 and 6252; and long-term gain or (loss) from Forms 4684, 6781, and 8824 . . . . . . **11**

12   Net long-term gain or (loss) from partnerships, S corporations, estates, and trusts from Schedule(s) K-1 . . . . **12**

13   Capital gain distributions. See page D-2 of the instructions **13**

14   Long-term capital loss carryover. Enter the amount, if any, from line 13 of your **Capital Loss Carryover Worksheet** on page D-7 of the instructions . . . . **14** ( )

15   **Net long-term capital gain or (loss).** Combine lines 8 through 14 in column (f). Then go to Part III on the back **15**

For Paperwork Reduction Act Notice, see Form 1040 or Form 1040NR instructions.   Cat. No. 11338H   Schedule D (Form 1040) 2008

Part III	Summary

16 Combine lines 7 and 15 and enter the result . . . . | **16** | |

If line 16 is:
- A **gain**, enter the amount from line 16 on Form 1040, line 13, or Form 1040NR, line 14. Then go to line 17 below.
- A **loss**, skip lines 17 through 20 below. Then go to line 21. Also be sure to complete line 22.
- **Zero**, skip lines 17 through 21 below and enter -0- on Form 1040, line 13, or Form 1040NR, line 14. Then go to line 22.

17 Are lines 15 and 16 **both** gains?
☐ **Yes.** Go to line 18.
☐ **No.** Skip lines 18 through 21, and go to line 22.

18 Enter the amount, if any, from line 7 of the **28% Rate Gain Worksheet** on page D-8 of the instructions . . . . ▶ | **18** | |

19 Enter the amount, if any, from line 18 of the **Unrecaptured Section 1250 Gain Worksheet** on page D-9 of the instructions . . . . ▶ | **19** | |

20 Are lines 18 and 19 **both** zero or blank?
☐ **Yes.** Complete Form 1040 through line 43, or Form 1040NR through line 40. Then complete the **Qualified Dividends and Capital Gain Tax Worksheet** on page 38 of the Instructions for Form 1040 (or in the Instructions for Form 1040NR). **Do not** complete lines 21 and 22 below.
☐ **No.** Complete Form 1040 through line 43, or Form 1040NR through line 40. Then complete the **Schedule D Tax Worksheet** on page D-10 of the instructions. **Do not** complete lines 21 and 22 below.

21 If line 16 is a loss, enter here and on Form 1040, line 13, or Form 1040NR, line 14, the **smaller** of:

- The loss on line 16 or
- ($3,000), or if married filing separately, ($1,500) } . . . . } | **21** | (|) |

Note. When figuring which amount is smaller, treat both amounts as positive numbers.

22 Do you have qualified dividends on Form 1040, line 9b, or Form 1040NR, line 10b?
☐ **Yes.** Complete Form 1040 through line 43, or Form 1040NR through line 40. Then complete the **Qualified Dividends and Capital Gain Tax Worksheet** on page 38 of the Instructions for Form 1040 (or in the Instructions for Form 1040NR).
☐ **No.** Complete the rest of Form 1040 or Form 1040NR.

This book contains information gleaned from many sources. This book is being published as a general reference and should not be used as a substitute for verification by users when warranted. The authors, licensees, nor the publishers are rendering any legal, financial, medical or psychological advice. They disclaim any personal liability, either directly or indirectly, for advice, personal opinions or contained information. Every effort was made to ensure the accuracy of this material; we assume no responsibility for errors, inaccuracies, omissions or any inconsistencies in the material. Errors concerning any person, place, publisher, book, organization, company or owner are strictly unintentional.